Forex for Beginners

The Best 10 Advice for Learning How to Make Money with Online Forex Trading and Create a Passive Income Working from Home

By

Simon Jordan

© **Copyright 2020 by Simon Jordan - All rights reserved.**

This document is geared towards providing exact and reliable information in regards to the topic and issue covered. The publication is sold with the idea that the publisher is not required to render accounting, officially permitted, or otherwise, qualified services. If advice is necessary, legal or professional, a practiced individual in the profession should be ordered.

- From a Declaration of Principles which was accepted and approved equally by a Committee of the American Bar Association and a Committee of Publishers and Associations.

In no way is it legal to reproduce, duplicate, or transmit any part of this document in either electronic means or in printed format. Recording of this publication is strictly prohibited and any storage of this document is not allowed unless with written permission from the publisher. All rights reserved.

The information provided herein is stated to be truthful and consistent, in that any liability, in terms of inattention or otherwise, by any usage or abuse of any policies, processes, or directions contained within is the solitary and utter responsibility of the recipient reader. Under no circumstances will any legal responsibility or blame be held against the publisher for any reparation, damages, or monetary loss due to the information herein, either directly or indirectly.

Respective authors own all copyrights not held by the publisher.

The information herein is offered for informational purposes solely, and is universal as so. The presentation of the information is without contract or any type of guarantee assurance.

The trademarks that are used are without any consent, and the publication of the trademark is without permission or backing by the trademark owner.

All trademarks and brands within this book are for clarifying purposes only and are the owned by the owners themselves, not affiliated with this document.

Table of Contents

INTRODUCTION 7

CHAPTER 1: AN INTRODUCTION TO THE WORLD OF FOREX TRADING 9

1.1 What Is Forex Trading? 9

1.2 Forex VS. Other Options of Trading 12

1.3 Forex Markets 15

1.4 The Key Terms Used in Forex Trading 17

1.5 Top 3 Platforms for Forex Trading 25

CHAPTER 2: UNDERSTANDING CURRENCY MOVEMENTS AND FACTORS AFFECTING IT 28

2.1 Defining Currency Movements 28

2.2 The Key Factors of Currency Rate Fluctuations 29

2.3 Effects of Macroeconomic Factors on Currency Movements 36

2.4 The Most Significant Economic Indicators of Currency Movements 40

2.5 Market Psychology and the Golden Rule of Economic Indicators 46

CHAPTER 3: ROLE OF OPTIMUM TIMING IN FOREX TRADING 48

3.1 The Importance of Timing in Forex Trading 48

3.2 The Optimum Time to Trade Forex 49

3.2 When Not to Trade Forex? 51

3.4 Forex Trading and the Time Frames 53

CHAPTER 4: GETTING STARTED WITH FOREX TRADING 56

4.1 Gathering the Important Information 56

4.2 Choosing A Forex Broker to Start With 57

4.3 Setting up An Account 60

4.4 Arranging the Money 60

4.5 Crucial Traits for a Successful Trade 62

CHAPTER 5: RISK MANAGEMENT IN FOREX TRADING 68

5.1 Understanding the Risks in Forex Trading 68

5.2 Evaluating the Risks 70

5.3 Coping Up with the Difficult Situations 70

5.4 Why Traders Lose Money? 73

CHAPTER 6: ANALYSIS TO PREDICT THE MARKET FLUCTUATIONS 75

6.1 Fundamental Analysis 75

6.2 Technical Analysis 80

CHAPTER 7: TIPS FOR MAXIMIZING THE PROFITS AND MINIMIZING THE LOSSES 85

7.1 Advice for the Newbies 85

7.2 Tips and Tricks for Advanced Forex Traders 87

CONCLUSION 92

Introduction

Forex Trading refers to exchanging one currency into another. The exchange of currencies is vital for the workings of the global economy. Goods produced in a country and sold in other countries also require conversion of currency. Understand, by way of example, that the widely known iPhone is assembled using components from at least five countries and is exported to no less than 90 countries. Given that Apple accounts for its earnings and pays dividends in US dollars, payments to suppliers and repatriation of profits will require almost one hundred separate foreign exchange transactions for only this one product! When extending this notion to the global economy as a whole, you begin to grasp the nature of currency trade.

In reality, average daily turnover now exceeds $5 trillion in the forex markets. Spot trading alone in the USD / EUR represents $400 billion – enough to earn it the designated status of most of the world's traded financial assets. By comparison, the combined NYSE and Nasdaq account for maybe $150 billion in the volume of daily equities. In the past few years, the volume of global foreign exchange has doubled while the value of investments has stagnated. Of course, this is not a comparison of apples to apples, but the point is that the forex market is massive.

In the meantime, retail forex penetration is minimal. As we will clarify in due course, while many stockbrokers, bond brokers, and options brokers are all household names now, retail forex brokers appear tiny and specialized. They have very little mark visibility outside the forex niche.

Strange to see, this paradox also explains the phenomenal retail forex growth over the last few years and the likely continuation of this development over the next decade.

Forex trading seems to have advanced from a dark corner of the financial world into the mainstream. A chance that the majority of individual investors have long ignored has been brought to the forefront, and the battle to profit from it has begun.

Chapter 1: An Introduction to the World of Forex Trading

Forex is a foreign-currency and foreign-exchange portmanteau. For a wide range of reasons, typically for trade, trading, or tourism, Foreign Exchange is converting one currency into another currency. The average was even more than $5.1 trillion in daily forex trading volume, as per the latest triennial report from the Bank for International Settlements, a global bank for national central banks. Not even all of the combined stock markets around the world come close to this. Yet what would it imply by that? Take a look at forex trading in the next chapters, and you will find some exciting trading opportunities which are not available with other investments.

1.1 What Is Forex Trading?

Just like stocks, currency can be traded based on what you think its value is (or where it is headed). But the significant difference with Forex trading is that you can swap just as quickly upwards or downwards. If you think that the value of a currency will increase, you can buy it. If you think it's going to decrease, then you can sell it. For such a broad market, it is much easier to find a buyer when you sell, and a seller when you buy in other countries. You may read in the papers that China is devaluing its currency to attract more foreign business into their country. If you think this trend will continue, by selling the Chinese currency against some other currency, say, the U.S. dollar, you could make a forex trade. The higher your profits will be when the Chinese currency devalues against the U.S. dollar. If the value of the Chinese currency increases while you have your selling position open, then your losses rise, and you want to get out of the particular trade.

Forex, or foreign Exchange, can be described as a network of buyers and sellers who move currency at an agreed price among themselves. It's how individuals, businesses, and central banks convert one currency into another – if you've ever traveled abroad, you've probably made a forex transaction.

Currencies are traded mostly in the foreign exchange market. For most people, currencies are relevant, since currencies need to be exchanged to conduct international trade and commerce. If you live in the U.S. and want to buy cheese from France, either you or the relevant company you buy cheese from has to pay the French in euros for the cheese. This means the U.S. importer has to swap the U.S. dollar equivalent value into euros. The same applies to travel. A French tourist in Egypt can't pay to see the pyramids in euros, because it's not the local currency. As such, the tourist has to swap the Euro at the local currency's current exchange rate.

One peculiar feature of this international market is that there is no central foreign-exchange marketplace. Today, currency trading is carried out electronically over-the-counter (OTC), meaning all transactions take place through communications networks amongst traders across the world, rather than through one centralized Exchange. The market operates 24 hours a day, five and a half days a week. Currencies are exchanged worldwide in London, New York, Tokyo, Zurich, Frankfurt, Hong Kong, Singapore, Paris, Sydney, and other major financial centers across almost every time zone. That means the forex market starts in Tokyo and Hong Kong when the U.S. trading day ends. As such, the forex market can be highly competitive every time of the day, with price quotes constantly changing.

Although a lot of foreign Exchange is performed for practical purposes, a large proportion of currency conversion is conducted to profit.

The amount of currency exchanged each day can make extremely unpredictable price fluctuations of certain currencies. This uncertainty can make Forex so appealing to traders: making high profits more possible and increasing the risk.

It is essential to practice in an environment as dynamic as the Forex properly. Whether you're a seasoned industry veteran or brand new to currency trading, being ready is key to successful profit-making.

That's a lot better said than done, of course. Your on-the-job preparation must never stop to ensure you have the best shot at forex success. In the fast-paced forex world, establishing robust trading strategies, joining expert webinars, and pursuing your market education are ways to stay competitive.

If your goal is to become a reliably successful forex trader, then you can never stop your education. As the adage goes, practice makes perfect; even for active traders, perfection is always elusive; it should be routine to be prepared for any session.

The Forex is the world's largest marketplace for money. Having a daily turnover of around $5 trillion, the Forex is a global trading platform where speculators, investors, and liquidity providers worldwide connect.

It is crucial to create an educational framework for those new to the global currency trade before jumping in with both feet. Comprehending the Forex's essential points is vital to getting up to speed as soon as possible. You must be able to read a quote, calculate leverage, and position orders on the market.

If you play the lottery, it's not an opportunity that you win. It takes desire, dedication, and aptitude to master any discipline. It's no different from becoming a winning forex trader. Your journey to the marketplace is very likely doomed before it begins without the want, will, and know-how.

Luckily, many of the dissimilarities between successful traders and money-losers are no longer a secret. With an intensive analysis of consumer behavior, you can find three places where the winning traders excel. Although there is no "holy grail" for successful forex trading, it is a great way to boost your performance by developing good habits in terms of risk vs. reward, leverage, and timing.

The average investment needed to start trading was about $10,000 by around 2002. Unlike other markets in finance today, Forex doesn't require a considerable budget for you to participate. Trading can be started with just $300-$ 500.

In contrast to the stock market with millions of different shares, Forex works with eight underlying currencies, the center of most trades. Also, there are considerably fewer factors that affect currency exchange rates than those in the stock market

A $50 billion market isn't just a miraculously beautiful number- it's also what makes sure you can sell or buy any amount of money you want at any time.

1.2 Forex VS. Other Options of Trading

Active investors and traders today have access to an increasing range of trading tools, from tried and tested blue-chip stocks to fast-paced futures and (or forex) foreign-exchange markets. Deciding which of these markets can be complicated to trade, and taking into account many factors makes the best choice.

The most significant element can be the risk tolerance and trading style of the trader or investor. Buy-and-hold investors, for example, are often more adapted to taking part in the stock market. At the same time, short-term traders — including swing, day, and scalp traders — may prefer Forex with more pronounced price volatility.

Forex Vs. Stocks

Often traders compare Forex vs. stocks to decide which market is better for trade. While being intertwined, the Forex and the stock market are varying considerably. The forex market has distinctive features that distinguish it from other markets and makes it much more attractive to trade in the eyes of many.

If deciding to trade Forex or stocks, it always includes determining which trading style best suits you. Understanding the stock and forex market variations and similarities often help traders make appropriate trading judgments based on factors like market conditions, liquidity, and duration.

The sheer scale of the forex market is one of the main disparities between Forex and stocks. Forex is expected to trade about $5 trillion per day, with most trade centered on a handful of big pairs such as EUR / USD, USD / JPY, GBP / USD, and AUD / USD. The forex market cap dwarfs the total dollar value of all capital markets around the world, which averages about $200 billion a day.

Having such a large volume of trading can bring a great many benefits to traders. High volume usually means traders can get their orders to be fulfilled quicker and closer to the rates they expect. While all markets are vulnerable to shortages, having more liquidity better equips traders to join and leave the market at each price point.

Generally, a high-volume trading market has high liquidity. Liquidity results in more tight spreads and lower transaction costs. Major Forex pairs typically have extremely low spreads and transaction costs when particularly in comparison to stocks, and this is one of the significant advantages of trading the forex market versus stock market trading.

Forex is an over-the-counter market, which means it is not transacted through a traditional exchange. It facilitates trading through the interbank market. That means trading can go on worldwide during business hours and trading sessions in different countries. So, the forex trader has access to trading almost 24 hours a day, five days a week. In contrast, major stock indices, trade at different times, and various variables affect them.

Most forex brokers charge no commission, instead make their spread margin – which is the difference among the selling price and the purchase price. When trading stocks, or a primary index such as the S&P 500, traders often have to pay a broker the spread along with a commission.

Forex spreads are relatively straightforward when compared with other contract trading prices. Below you can see the EUR / USD gap outlined inside the executable prices of the dealing. The spread can be used upfront before execution to calculate the cost for your position size.

There are eight major currencies that traders can focus on, while there are thousands in the stock universe. With only eight economies to focus on and as Forex is traded in pairs, traders will look for currency-to-currency diverging and converging trends to match a forex pair to trade. Eight currencies are better than thousands of inventories to keep an eye on.

Using an economic calendar, the variables that affect the major currencies can be monitored easily.

Internet and electronic commerce have opened the doors for active traders and investors worldwide to participate in an increasing variety of markets. For certain situations, the judgment to trade stocks, Forex, or futures contracts is based on risk appetite, portfolio size, and comfort.

If there is no active trader available to enter, exit, or adequately handle trades during regular market hours, stocks are not the best choice. Nonetheless, if a business strategy for an investor is to buy and hold on a long-term basis, producing steady growth and collecting dividends, stocks are a realistic option. The instrument(s) chosen by a trader or investor should be based on which strategies, objectives, and risk tolerance fit best.

1.3 Forex Markets

The forex market is genuinely new, as we understand it today. Of course, in its most basic sense, people converting one currency for financial advantage to another, Forex has been around since nations started minting currencies. But modern forex markets are a fashionable invention. Following the 1971 Bretton Woods agreement, more major currencies were permitted to float freely at each other. Specific currency values vary, which has contributed to the need for foreign exchange facilities and trading.

Investment and commercial banks conduct most trading on behalf of their clients in the forex markets. Still, there are also speculative opportunities for professional and individual investors to trade one currency against another.

Also, there are three ways companies, businesses, and individuals exchange forexes: the spot market, the forward market, and the futures market. Spot-market forex trading has always been the most significant market since it is the "underlying" real asset on which forward and futures markets are based. The futures market has been the most popular venue for traders in the past because it has been accessible to investors for a longer time.

However, with both the emergence of computer trading and countless forex brokers, the spot market has witnessed an enormous increase in activity and now exceeds the futures market as the preferred market for individual investors and speculators. When people often refer to the forex market, they usually refer to the spot market. The forward and futures markets appear to be more familiar with businesses that need to hedge their future foreign exchange risks to a specific date.

Specifically, the spot market is also where currencies are purchased and sold at the current price. This level, calculated by supply and demand, represents several factors, including current interest rates, economic growth, sentiment towards ongoing political situations, plus the perception of one currency's potential success against another.

This is known as a "spot deal" when a deal is finalized. It is a bilateral transaction through which one party delivers an agreed-upon currency amount to the counterpart and collects a fixed amount of another currency at the agreed-upon exchange rate value. The settlement is in cash after a place is closed. Although the spot market is widely regarded as one that deals with current (rather than future) transactions, these trades generally take two days for settlement.

In contrast to the spot market, the futures and forwards markets do not trade real currencies. Instead, they deal with contracts representing claims to a particular type of currency, a specific price per unit, and a future settlement date.

OTC contracts are purchased and sold between two parties in the forward market, which determines the terms of the agreement among themselves.

In the futures market, futures contracts are purchased and sold on public commodity markets, such as the Chicago Mercantile Exchange, based on a standard size and settling date.

The National Futures Association regulates the market for the future in the U.S. Futures contracts contain specific details, which include the number of units being traded, the dates of delivery and settlement, and the minimum price increases, which cannot be customized. The Exchange acts as the trader's counterpart, providing clearance and settlement.

Both types of contracts are binding and are typically settled for cash upon expiry at the Exchange in question, though contracts can also be purchased and sold before they expire. Markets forwards and futures will provide risk protection when trading currencies. Big foreign companies typically use these markets to protect against potential volatility in exchange rates, but speculators often invest in those markets.

1.4 The Key Terms Used in Forex Trading

The Forex business comes with a particular range of words and jargon. Before you go deeper into understanding how to trade the Forex market, it's essential to understand some of the simple Forex jargon you'll find on your business venture.

Here's a list of the most vital terminologies used in forex trading:

Exchange Rate:

A currency pair's exchange rate is what all traders obey. The exchange rate is often simply referred to as the price since it shows the base currency price expressed in terms of the counter currency. For instance, if the EUR / USD exchange rate is 1.15, it will take $1.15 to purchase one Euro.

A rise in a currency pair's exchange rate shows that the base currency appreciates against the counter-currency, or the counter-currency depreciates against the base currency.

Likewise, a decline in the exchange rate illustrates that the base currency depreciates against the counter-currency, or that the counter-currency appreciates the base currency.

Currency:

Currency is the money used as a circulating medium, such as banknotes and coins. Some sources refer to currencies as a money-system used among a nation's people.

Currently, the United Nations recognizes 180 currencies that are used worldwide in 195 countries. A few examples of currencies are the U.S. dollar, the Euro, the British pound and the Japanese yen, all of which act as value stores and are traded on the global foreign exchange (Forex) market.

As with other assets, the supply and demand forces determine a currency's value relative to another currency. Increased currency supply sinks its value, while increased demand pushes its value upwards.

Cross Rate:

The exchange rate of currency amongst two currencies, although both are not the official currencies of the country where the quote for the exchange rate is given in. This phrase has sometimes been used to refer to currency quotes that do not include the U.S. dollar, irrespective of which country the quote is provided.

Currency Pair:

We cannot buy or sell single currencies even though currencies are traded on the Forex market. We have to trade on currency pairs each time we place a trade in the market. Currency pairs consist of two currencies: the first is the base currency, and the second is the counter currency.

One example of a currency pair is the pair EUR / USD. When we buy the EUR / USD pair, we obtain the Euro and sell the dollar for the U.S. In the same way, when we sell the EUR / USD pair, we sell the Euro and buy the U.S. dollar.

Leverage:

Strictly speaking, the forex broker lends you money by leverage so that you can exchange larger lots:

Leverage is a feature of the broker and its versatility. At the same time, leverage can vary 100:1, 200:1, or even 500:1. You can use $1,000 to exchange $100,000 (1,000100) or $200,000 (1,000200), or $500,000 (1,000500) with leverage.

First, it depends upon the type of account you open, what the leverage is, and how much leverage you need for that specific type of account. Don't be selfish – but also don't be too quiet. Leverage can be used to optimize profits-but losses can also be used if you are too greedy.

Firstly, your broker would need an initial margin on your account, which is to say a minimum deposit.

You open a trading account which has a 1:100 leverage. You want to sell a $500,000 place, but you have just $5,000 in your account. No worries, your broker is going to lend you the remaining $495,000 and set aside $5,000 as your deposit of good faith.

The gains you gain from investing will be added to the account balance-or they will be deducted if there are losses. Leverage increases your purchasing power and will triple your winnings and losses.

Also, choose a broker that does not provide any insurance against negative balance, so your losses will never surpass your money. It means that if your loss hits USD 5,000, your positions will be immediately closed, so you don't end up owing your broker money.

Cross Pairs and Exotics:

On the other hand, cross pairs comprise any two significant currencies except the U.S. dollar. Cross-pairs, unlike big pairs, have higher transaction costs, and traders can face slippage in periods of lower liquidity. Cross-pairs are usually more volatile than large pairs as well. Cross-paired examples include EUR / GBP, EUR / CHF and AUD / NZD.

Finally, exotic pairs usually involve exotic currencies, not in the top 10 of the most frequently traded currencies, such as with the Mexican peso, Turkish lira, or Czech Coruna. Because those currencies can be highly volatile, the pros should be left to deal with them.

Bid Price/Ask Price:

Every currency pair has two exchange rates at any given moment, the bid price, and the requested price. Which is the difference between the two? The bid price is usually the price at which buyers are willing to purchase, while the asking price is the price at which sellers are interested in selling.

Despite its existence, the bid price is always lower than the asking price. Once those two prices cross, either when sellers lower their ask price to match a buyer's bid price or when buyers raise their cost, they're willing to pay for a currency to meet a seller's asking price, a transaction occurs.

Ultimately buyers buy at the price of the ask, and sellers sell at the price of the offer. It means that each price plotted on your chart reflects the equilibrium price at that particular time – the price at which the large percentage of market players are willing to transact.

Margin:

The deposit needed for opening or maintaining a place. Margin can either be 'free' or 'used.'

The margin used is the amount used to maintain an open position, whereas the free margin is the respective amount available to open new positions. You can purchase or sell a position worth a notional $100,000 with a $1,000 margin balance and a one percent margin requirement to open a position. This allows a trader to leverage up to 100 times his account, or a leverage ratio of 100:1.

When a trader's account falls below the minimum sum needed to retain an open position, a "margin call" will be given, forcing him to either add more money to his or her account or close the open position. Many brokers close a trade automatically when the margin balance falls below the amount required to hold it open. The amount needed to maintain an open position depends on the broker and could amount to 50 percent of the original margin required to open the trade.

Spread:

You have to pay transaction fees for the trade every time you participate in a trade. Although most brokers nowadays do not charge fees and commissions on placing orders, the bid / ask spread remains the key expense to Forex traders. If bulls buy at the ask price, their position is in a loss instantly equal to the spread of the bid/offer.

If you're a day trader, you have to pay attention to the bid / ask spread because they can eat a large fraction of your profits. The spread fewer impacts swing traders and position traders with a longer-term trading approach since they open up fewer positions and have comparatively high-profit targets.

Lots:

This term is commonly used when trading derivatives on the Forex markets. Forex futures contracts on the market often have a fixed duration.

U.S. dollar contracts, for example, may be offered in multiples of $5000. And every $5000 contract would be called a number. So, if you want to acquire USD 25,000 in the future, you'll need to buy five lots. Various currencies are available in different lot sizes. Market makers offer currencies that have higher liquidity more flexibility.

Pip:

When thinking about gains or losses, Forex traders typically use the word "pips." A pip is short of Percentage in Point and reflects the smallest movement. An exchange rate will shift upwards or downwards. Usually, the fourth integer value of most currency pairs is equated with one pip.

For example, if EUR / USD currently trades at 1.1558 and rises to 1.1562, the increase will be equivalent to a 4-pip shift. Many currency pairs, however, have their pips in second decimal position, often yen-pairs. If USD / JPY currently trades at 110.25 and starts falling to 110.10, that drop would be equivalent to a 15-pip change.

Pipette:

A pip is the fourth decimal point of most currency pairs, but there is also an even smaller increase that can change prices. This is called pipette and is equal to 1/10 of a pip, i.e., ten pipettes are one pip. A pipette is in the fifth decimal position in most pairs (they are in the third decimal place of yen-pairs)

Most traders don't follow pipette movements, although some brokers use them on their trading platform. Pipettes are mostly used today to measure the spread of bid/ask, where a tenth of a pip is required. For instance, the EUR / USD spread might be 1.4 pips, or one pip and four pipettes.

Execution:

It is the order-completion process.

Once you have placed your order, the order will be forwarded to your broker, who wants to fill it out, deny it, or quote it again. When your order is filled out, your broker will give you a confirmation.

Getting the instructions followed rapidly is essential. When your order is delayed, it can cause you losses. That's why in less than 1 second, your forex broker should also be able to execute orders. Forex is a fast-moving market – and often forex brokers don't keep up with its speed, or purposely slow down execution to snatch a few pips from you though during slow market movements.

Going Long/Short:

You have probably heard in a currency pair about going long or short. Going long merely means buying while going short means selling. Most traders are long in equity markets in expectation of rising prices. Nevertheless, there is still an equal number of longs and shorts on the market in financial markets, like options and futures, since each new contract that is bought has a corresponding seller who wants to go short, and vice versa.

Because Forex retail is often traded with CFDs, traders can bet on rising prices and falling prices. They go "long" when buying, and when they short-sell, they go "short."

Support:

Help and resistance are among the most critical technical and analytical concepts. Technical traders only analyze price movements as they believe the price reflects the necessary data, and support and resistance trading play a significant role in this analysis.

The markets are made up of crowds of people who bet on the economy, hedge, sell, save, or gamble. Because people have memories, they recall certain price levels where in the past, the price had trouble breaking down.

They put their buy orders around those rates, assuming that the price would fail to break down again below. This is how levels of support are formed. In other words, a level of support is a previous low at which the price has a great chance to retrace and push upwards.

Resistance:

Like support levels, resistance levels are also a crucial tool in the toolbox of a technical trader. Although support levels are based on past lows, rates of resistance follow previous peaks at which the price was having trouble breaking above.

Traders recall those rates and put their selling orders around them because they expect those rates will again generate the selling pressure, and the price is pushed down. Because fresh memory is more essential than old memory, the new levels of support and resistance are typically more important than early levels of support and resistance.

Value dates and Rollovers:

The value date is the date the trading parties agree to fix their accounts. This ensures that derivative contracts' open positions are immediately closed on the date of the interest. Consequently, contracts become much more volatile once they are closer to the date of value.

For some instances, traders often agree to turn their contracts over. It means that instead of the present value date, they decide to settle their contracts until the next value date. To do so, both the parties must agree, and then fees must also be paid as per the difference in interest rates between the two currencies.

1.5 Top 3 Platforms for Forex Trading

The global foreign exchange (Forex) market is by far the world's largest and most actively traded financial market. When looking for the "best" forex broker, beginners, as well as seasoned traders, are usually looking for many main features and advantages among the most significant are: overall trading experience, product selection and scope (currencies, CFDs, indices, cryptocurrencies, etc.), fees (such as spreads and commissions), trading platforms (web-based, interactive software, internet, charting and third-party platforms), customer service, trading education, and study, and trust woods.

Through comprehensive research and strict adherence to our rigorous methodology, we have found the best forex brokers in all these areas and more, resulting in our top rankings in the following regions. The mission has always been to allow people to make the most informed choices about how to trade, when, and where to invest. Considering the recent market uncertainty and developments in the online forex brokerage industry, we are dedicated to providing our readers with objective and expert reviews of the best trading platforms for all kinds of traders, for every type of sector.

CMC Markets: The Best Market Overall and Best for The Range of Offerings

Set up in 1989, CMC Markets (CMC) is a well-established, publicly traded, and highly regarded U.K. Forex broker which has adapted successfully to the always-changing online brokerage landscape. The company is listed under the ticker symbol CMCX, on the London Stock Exchange (LSE). As with many forex brokers, CMC does not accept American traders.

CMC Markets is for almost all types of traders, from novice retailers looking to dip their toes into Forex, CFDs and spread betting online trading arenas to experienced veterans looking for exposure to a wide range of products. Fees for the company are competitive within the industry and rank high on several of today's lists.

Saxo Capital Markets: The Best Market for Advanced Traders

Founded in 1992, Denmark's Saxo Bank Group (Saxo Bank) classifies itself as "a leading Fintech specialist focusing on multi-asset trading and investment and providing 'Banking-as-a-Service' to wholesale clients." The company welcomed the technological innovations of the late 1990s when it launched one of the first electronic trading platforms in 1998. Saxo Bank has existed in the U.K. via its subsidiary Saxo Capital Markets U.K. Ltd (SCML) since 2006 and, like other forex brokers, does not accept U.S. traders.

For the professional investor, Saxo Capital Markets were. It provides a broad range of brokerage services targeted at sophisticated, active traders, customers, practitioners, and institutions. Relatively small account holders will encounter several unexpected hurdles, including higher account minimum, a variety of fees, and fewer options for customer support. Tiered accounts reduce selling costs and add advantages as equity grows, but most retailers will have a hard time hitting the higher consumer rates

XTB Online Trading: Best Platform for Low-Cost Trading

Established in 2002 as the first leveraged foreign exchange brokerage house in Poland, in 2004, X-Trade morphed into X-Trade Brokers to comply with new Polish regulations. Then, in 2009, it rebranded its current incarnation, XTB Online Trading (XTB), and went public, listing under the ticker symbol XTB on the Warsaw Stock Exchange in 2016. The organization does not allow traders in the U.S.

XTB is a sound choice for traders wishing to minimize their costs, whether it is the inherent cost of placing a trade or not having to be burdened with external costs, such as wire charges. For non-U.K. XTB provides full flexibility up to 500:1. Though the U.K. accounts, Accounts have equity of up to 30:1. The company emphasizes customer support and provides relevant educational tools and research attractions that would fit a novice trader well.

Chapter 2: Understanding Currency Movements and Factors Affecting it

The forex market consists of currencies from around the world, making forecasts of exchange rates challenging because several variables could lead to price movements. Nonetheless, as with most financial markets, forex is driven primarily by supply and demand forces, and it's vital to be aware of the factors that drive price fluctuations here.

2.1 Defining Currency Movements

Investment markets will easily take the money from investors who think it is easy to trade. Trading is extraordinarily tricky in any investment sector, but success comes first with preparation and practice.

The currency market, or forex market, is the world's largest investment market and continues to expand every year. The forex market hit a daily average turnover of $4 trillion in April 2010, a rise of 20 percent since 2007.

On the contrary, the New York Stock Exchange has a daily turnover of just $25 billion. The market may be significant, but the volume came from professional traders until recently. As currency trading platforms have improved with time, more retail traders have found forex suited for their investment goals.

Currency trading is a massive 24-hour market that is only closed from Friday night until Sunday night, but the 24-hour trading sessions are deceptive. There are three hours, which comprise trading hours in Europe, Asia, and the United States.

While the sessions overlap slightly, the key currencies in each market are often exchanged during those market hours. It means that there would be more volatility in some currency pairs at specific sessions. Traders remaining with dollar-based pairs should find the most value in the U.S. trading session.

Currency is traded in lots of varying scales. The micro-lot is a currency of 1000 units. When your account is supported in U.S. dollars, your base currency, the Dollar, is represented by a micro number. A mini lot is your base currency's 10,000 units, and a regular batch is 100,000 units.

Just two forex triggers do exist supply and demand. All of these, in effect, are motivated by one thing: emotion. Nonetheless, the sentiment is influenced by an endless number of factors. The investor mood is particularly sensitive to the flow of news, information, and other trends around the world, mainly because the fast-moving forex market goes up 24 hours a day.

2.2 The Key Factors of Currency Rate Fluctuations

Many stock traders are becoming interested in currency markets because the currency market is also driven by many of the forces that move the stock market. One of the largest of these is supply and demand. If the world wants more money, the Dollar's value rises, and the price falls because so many are circulated.

Other variables, such as interest rates, the latest economic data from the major countries, and global tensions, are only a few events that might influence currency prices.

All trading of currencies is performed in pairs. Unlike the stock market, where you can simply buy or sell a single stock, you have to buy one currency in the forex market and sell another currency. First, almost every currency is priced out to the fourth decimal point. The smallest rise in trade is a pip or percentage point. One pip is usually 1/100 of 1%. Retail or beginning traders often exchange currency in micro lots, since one pip in a micro lot represents just a 10-cent change in price. This makes it easier to handle losses when a transaction fails to achieve the expected results. One pip in a mini lot is $1, and the same one pip in a regular lot is $10. Some currencies in a single trading session jump as much as 100 pips or more, making the possible losses to the small investor far more manageable through dealing in micro or mini lots.

The bulk of currency trading volume is limited to only 18 currency pairs relative to the thousands of stocks listed on the global equity markets. The eight currencies most commonly exchanged are the U.S. dollar (USD), Canadian dollar (CAD), euro (EUR), British pound (GBP), Swiss franc (CHF), New Zealand dollar (NZD), Australian dollar (AUD) and Japanese yen (JPY). However, there are many exchanged pairs outside of the 18. While no one can say that trading in currencies is secure, having much less trading options makes trading and portfolio management simpler.

Through the years, the players' impact in the F.X. market has changed. Traditionally, importers and exporters of goods were the leading players on the F.X. markets, exchanging currencies through banks. Therefore foreign exchange became the primary producer of currency supply and demand. Trade also directly affects F.X. Markets through trade, and indirectly through market fluctuations that follow official data on foreign trade and investment flow. Yet over time, trade's significance has diminished as financial investors are becoming more involved in F.X. markets.

The driving force behind this shift to a market dominated by foreigners has been the quest for lucrative cross-border investment opportunities. For, e.g., by keeping shares in U.S. dollars, a British investor buying U.S. equities takes on currency risk. To insulate income from the effects of any adverse changes in the exchange rate, the investor may want to hedge this risk.

Investors have discovered currencies in recent years as a distinct asset class, and potentially an additional source of profits. Higher returns on conventional asset groups, such as equities and bonds, and a gap between the assets and potential pension fund liabilities prompted investors to search for new, uncorrelated sources of return. Currencies can bring not only diversification but the potential for incremental returns due to F.X. market inefficiencies.

Financial firms are the F.X. market's biggest competitors. According to the Bank for Foreign Settlements, interbank business accounts for around half of F.X. turnover. Still, the most significant growth in participation comes from individual financial institutions, including insurance firms, hedge funds, pension funds, asset managers, and central banks.

Exchange Rate Determinants:

Various factors calculate exchange rates. Many of those factors are linked to the two countries' trade relationship. Note, the exchange rates are relative and are presented as a contrast between two countries ' currencies. Several of the critical determinants of the exchange rate between the two countries are as follows. Remember that these factors are in no specific order; like other economics, there is much discussion about the relative significance of those factors.

Inflation:

A country with a lower inflation rate usually experiences a rising currency value, as its buying power increases compared to other currencies. During the second half of the 20th century, low-inflation countries included Germany, Japan, and Switzerland, while the U.S. and Canada experienced low inflation only later. Those countries with higher inflation usually saw their trading partners' currencies depreciating in their currencies. Typically, that also comes with higher interest rates.

Interest Rates:

Interest rate adjustments impact currency value and exchange rate for the Dollar. Both of these are associated with forex prices, interest rates, and inflation. The rise in interest rates causes the nation's currency to rise, as low-interest rates have better prices for borrowers, drawing more foreign capital, leading to an increase in exchange rates.

All of these are closely correlated with interest rates, inflation, and exchange rates. Central banks gain control across both inflation and exchange rates by manipulating interest rates, and inflation and currency values are impacted by changing interest rates. Higher interest rates give a better return for the borrowers in an economy relative to other nations. Higher interest rates, therefore, draw international capital and trigger a rise in the exchange rate. The effect of rising interest rates is mitigated when inflation is far higher in the country than in others, or when additional factors help to push down the currency. There is the reverse trend with high-interest rates- that is, lower interest rates lead to lower exchange rates.

Current Account Deficits:

A current account is the trade balance between a country and its trading partners, representing all payments for goods, services, interest, and dividends between countries. A current account deficit shows that the nation spends more on foreign exchange than it receives and borrows money from outside sources to make the difference. In other words, the nation needs more foreign currency than it earns from export sales, and it produces more of its currency than the demand from foreigners for its goods. Excess demand for foreign currency reduces the nation's exchange rate until local services and products are affordable enough for outsiders, and foreign assets are too costly for domestic interests to generate sales.

The current account of a nation represents the trade balance and foreign investment profits. It consists of total transaction numbers, including exports, imports, debt, etc. A current account deficit due to more of its money being expended on buying goods than it receives from export sales creates depreciation. The balance of payments fluctuates with the domestic currency exchange rate.

Public Debt:

Countries must participate in large-scale deficit financing to pay for policy and public sector programs. While such activity boosts the domestic economy, nations with high government deficits and debts are less attractive to investors. A significant debt causes inflation, and if the rise is high, the debt will be serviced and finally paid off in the future with cheaper real dollars.

In the worst-case scenario, a government might print money to pay part of a huge debt, but it eventually induces inflation to raise the money supply. Moreover, suppose a government cannot fund its debt through domestic means (selling domestic bonds, raising the supply of money). In that case, it must increase the supply of securities for sale to outsiders, thus lowering their prices. Finally, a considerable debt may be troubling to outsiders if they conclude that the country risks defaulting on its obligations. When the probability of default increases, investors would be less likely to buy securities denominated in that currency. For this reason, the country's debt rating (as calculated, for example, by Moody's or Standard & Poor's) is a crucial determinant of their exchange rate.

Terms of Trade:

The terms of exchange relating to the current accounts and the balance of payments are the ratio of export prices with import prices. Trade conditions for a country improve as its export prices increase at a higher rate than its import prices. This results in increased sales, resulting in increased demand for the nation's currency and a rise in the value of its currency, which results in an exchange-rate appreciation.

A ratio of export prices and import prices, trade rates are linked to current accounts and balance of payments. When a country's export price increases at a higher rate than its imports, its trading conditions have changed favorably. Increasing terms of the increased demand for the country's exports from trade shows. This, in effect, results in increasing export sales, creating an increased demand for the currency of the nation (and an increase in the value of the currency). When the export price increases at a slower rate than imports, the value of the currency in comparison to its trading partners would decrease.

Political Performance and Stability:

The political situation and economic performance of a country can greatly influence the strength of its currency. A country with less potential for political instability is more feasible for foreign investors, resulting in greater political and economic stability, attracting investment away from other countries. In addition, an increase in foreign capital results in an appreciation of the value of its local currency. A country with a sound financial and trade policy does not give its currency any room for uncertainty. But a country vulnerable to political instability may see exchange rate depreciation.

International investors will eventually be searching for prosperous countries with good economic growth to invest their money in. A nation with these positive characteristics would attract foreign funds away from other perceived political and economic risk-taking countries. For example, political instability may cause a lack of confidence in a currency and a capital transfer to the currencies of more stable countries.

Recession:

If a nation enters a recession, the interest rates are expected to decline, reducing the prospects of foreign capital acquisitions. As a result, the currency weakens compared to those of other countries, thereby raising the exchange rate.

Speculation:

When the currency value of a nation is projected to rise, investors will be seeking more of that currency to generate a profit in the immediate future. As a consequence, the currency's value will increase because of increasing demand. There also comes an improvement in the exchange rate for this rise in currency value.

The currency exchange rate at which a portfolio stores the majority of its investments decides the actual return. A falling exchange rate naturally reduces the buying power of any returns on dividends and capital gains. The exchange rate also affects other revenue variables such as interest rates, inflation, and even domestic stock capital gains. Although exchange rates are decided by various influencing factors that often leave even the most skilled economists baffled, investors should still have an understanding of how exchange rates and currency values play an essential part in the rate of return on the investment.

All these factors decide the fluctuations in the foreign exchange rate. If you frequently send or receive money, being up-to-date about these factors will help you better assess the optimum time for overseas money transfer. To prevent future fall in currency exchange rates, look for a locked-in exchange rate contract to ensure that your currency is traded at the same rate amid any factors causing an unfavorable fluctuation.

2.3 Effects of Macroeconomic Factors on Currency Movements

Forex is a real global economy, with sellers and buyers from all regions of the world taking part in trillions of trade dollars every day. The acknowledgment that foreign exchange trading is becoming such a global operation means that macroeconomic developments are playing a significant role in forex anywhere. Traders no longer have to stick to conventional currencies, but they are a strong starting point. Below are some economic developments and events which will enable those new to the market to become effective forex traders.

The Role of Macroeconomics in Forex:

The forex market is driven mainly by paramount macroeconomic factors. Such factors affect the decisions made by a trader and eventually decide the value of the currency at any given time. The economic stability of the economy of a country is a critical factor in their currency exchange rate. Economic overall health can change rapidly, based on current affairs and new data. However, most of the best forex traders are highly disciplined and adhere to a set of trade guidelines. Let's have a closer look at a few of the factors that affect the positioning of an economy and drive shifts in its currency's value.

Capital Markets:

Among the most apparent indicators of health for an economy are the global capital markets. The dissemination of public knowledge of capital markets is easy to find. There is a steady supply of media reporting, as well as up-to-the-second knowledge about business, governmental, and government dealings. A rally or sell-off of shares from one country to another would be a strong indication that the economic outlook has changed for that economy.

Likewise, other economies are sector-driven, including the commodity-based economy in Canada. The Canadian Dollar is closely associated with resources, such as crude oil and metals.2 A rise in oil prices will possibly contribute to the Canadian Dollar's appreciation compared to other currencies. Commodity traders, like forex traders, rely heavily on their trades on the economic data. For certain cases, the same data will impact both markets directly. Trading correlations between currencies and commodities is a fascinating topic.

The bond markets are equally important to what's going on in the forex market as both fixed-income securities as well as currencies depend heavily on interest rates. Treasury price fluctuations are mostly a factor in exchange-rate changes, meaning a rise in yields can influence currency values directly. Therefore, to excel as a forex trader is necessary to understand bonds, and particularly government bonds.

International Trade:

The critical factor is the trade equilibrium among nations. The trade balance acts as a proxy for a country's relative demand for products. A nation with internationally high desired goods or services will usually see a currency appreciation. For example, if buyers want to purchase products from Australia, they must turn their money into Australian dollars. The rising demand for the Australian Dollar would drive its value upwards.

Countries with significant trade deficits, by comparison, are net buyers of imported goods. Much of their currency is sold to buy other nations' currencies to pay for foreign goods. This form of scenario would likely have a negative effect on the value of the currency of an importing nation.

Political News:

The political climate plays a critical role in a country's economic outlook, and ultimately, its currency's perceived value. Forex traders actively track political news and developments in order to predict changes in the national governments' economic policies. This may involve changes in government spending, and regulatory modifications levied on specific sectors or industries. Changes in the margin or leverage laws open to traders can have drastic market impacts.

Elections that have unpredictable outcomes are often critical events for currency markets. Exchange rates also respond favorably to wins from groups that are pro-growth or fiscally responsible. Even a vote may have a huge effect on the exchange rates. A perfect example of this is the Brexit referendum, which, when the U.K. voted to leave the E.U, had a drastic impact on the British pound.

Any government's fiscal and monetary policies are the most important elements in its economic decision-making. The forex market is keenly monitoring central bank decisions that affect interest rates for any major rate adjustments or policymakers' future outlook.

Economic Statistics:

Economic reports form the foundation of a playbook for a forex trader. Maintaining a schedule for an economic study is essential to keeping up to date in this fast-paced industry. Gross domestic product (GDP) can be the most recognizable economic statistics, as it is the basis for the economic success and strength of a country. GDP calculates the overall production of the manufactured goods and services within an economy. Yet understanding that GDP is a lagging measure is important. Which means it is reporting on events and developments that have already taken place.

Inflation is also a significant predictor because it sends out a warning of rising price rates and declining purchasing power. Inflation is a double edge knife, however. Some see it as imposing inflationary pressure on the currency, owing to the rising buying power. Inflation can also trigger currency appreciation, as it can push central banks to boost rates to combat rising levels of inflation. Inflation among economists is a fiercely debated topic, and its impact on currencies is seldom straightforward.

Employment rates, retail prices, manufacturing indices, and capacity utilization also bear valuable information about an economy's actual and expected strength and currency.

2.4 The Most Significant Economic Indicators of Currency Movements

Various governmental and non-governmental organizations around the world report periodically, with some pieces of economic details. The methods by which such reports are drawn up will vary greatly. The data is often as straightforward as recording monthly revenues from a different sector of the economy. Others can not originate from hard data but rather from opinions reported in surveys. Some can also derive their conclusions from the extrapolation of existing data.

Some indicators may remind you of the current economic state, while others will affirm what the economy has done before, and others will forecast what is yet to come. The final collection – known as the leading economic indicators – is of particular interest to traders, as it provides the strongest insight into the possible course of potential economic activities. The measures of the present state of the economy are called 'coincident.' Someone who confirms what has already happened is regarded as lagging indicators.

These indicators have their applications, which can have various impacts on the Forex market.

The biggest problem for traders who are just starting out is understanding which are the most important ones – the ones that are more likely to influence prices – and the ones are low impact. Such information is useful because there can be multiple economic indicators published in a single day, so keeping an eye on them all is not really theoretically feasible. We've put together an informative list of Forex economic indicators to try and help in this area.

We have included in our economic indicators list those which are considered to be the most relevant. All this has the potential to have a significant impact on the capital markets. Considering that the U.S. economy is the world's largest economy and exerts some impact on financial market results worldwide, our list focuses on U.S. data in an attempt to provide you with the best economic indicators.

Gross Domestic Product (GDP):

GDP is the indicator of an economy's overall safety. It takes such an extended period of time to compile that its direct impact on Forex and CFD prices is often muted – and many of the components are already known by the time the data is released, and therefore forecasts are still relatively correct. That said, should the number appear substantially differing from expectations, it still has the power to push the market.

It is a crucial factor to be taken into consideration, given its lack of timeliness, as it is the best measure used to validate where we are in the business cycle.

To modern economics, the market cycle is a central term. This consists of a period of growth, with multiple sectors of the economy increasing at the same time and a period of contraction when economic activity contracts. Since economic activity's broadest gage is GDP, economists prefer to assess where we're in the economic cycle by looking at alternations of GDP growth and contraction.

Two successive quarters of contraction in GDP is the statistical concept of a recession. As long as we see a quarter of growth, a recession stops. Politicians, economists, and economic analysts are all very much based on this metric, primarily because it is such a detailed measure. Investment banks will begin by making forecasts for the general economic climate by adopting a top-down approach to the Forex analysis. GDP is a vital part of this sort of macroeconomic study of the foreign exchange market.

We need to be aware of it as well as experienced traders, but you should also be aware of the fact that since GDP is a lagging indicator, its main use is to validate what we already predict. Its lack of timeliness means its usefulness as a resource for short- and medium-term trading is minimal. US GDP comes out about once a quarter, and only the earliest calculation goes back into the past few months.

Unemployment Rate:

The unemployment rate is classified as the percentage of the labor force, which actively seeks work. Unemployment serves as a laggard measure in times of recovery. Traders expect to see a continuing rise in unemployment long after GDP has bottomed out. There is also a strong correlation between unemployment and consumer sentiment. Extended periods of unemployment are particularly detrimental to consumer sentiment, and can often affect consumer spending and economic growth.

Unemployment data provides CFD traders with insights into one of the main indicators that the FED implements. This means any sharp deviation from expectations is likely to have a significant effect on Forex markets. All things being equal, the weakening of the U.S. labor market will be deemed historically as bearish for stock markets and the U.S. dollar.

Consumer Price Index (CPI):

The CPI calculates the costs of the goods and services, indexed to a starting point for the foundation. It gives us unbiased handling of how quickly markets go up or down. As we already discussed in the article, price stability is part of the dual mandate of the FED. It is considered natural, or even desirable when inflation is below target levels. If inflation goes too far off target for too long, however, it can have very negative economic impacts.

FED economists tend to concentrate on the PCE price index, which is included in the GDP survey. That's published only quarterly, so Forex and CFD traders mostly follow the CPI as it's a timelier inflation tracker. The usefulness of the CPI as a leading economic indicator is minimal. Given a natural and rational correlation between economic growth, demand, and higher prices, it has proved to be a weak indicator of turning points in the business cycle.

High inflation was a major problem for the U.S. economy during the 1970s and early 1980s. In comparison, there was a great danger of deflation in the wake of the global financial crisis (sustained price decreases). Deflation affects the economy by motivating customers to avoid buying because, in the future, they will be cheaper as long as prices continue to fall. It would hinder economic growth because consumer spending represents such a large part of the GDP, which can create a vicious cycle.

Since inflation feeds so directly into monetary policy, the CPI report will strongly influence bond, F.X., and stock market prices. As normal, the highest effect appears to be the distractions from planned outcomes. For example, if CPI comes in much higher than expected, the view that the FED will be more likely to ease monetary policy in the future will be shifted. It would be positive for the U.S. dollar, all things being equal.

Likewise, these inflationary data may be viewed by a CFD investor as bearish for the stock market, as stricter monetary policy aims to curb risk appetite. We've been in a very low inflationary climate since the financial crisis, which has pressured the Federal Reserve to stick to very loose monetary policy. It has been responsible for the expanded bull market we've seen in the U.S. to some degree.

Industrial Production Index:

The Industrial Production Index calculates the level of U.S. production (in terms of quantity of material produced rather than the sum of Dollar) compared to a base year in three-wide areas: manufacturing, mining, and gas and electrical utilities. The Federal Reserve compiles the study, which is released in the middle of the month. Most of the index data come from hard data, published directly by trade associations or official surveys for other sectors, although this may not always be available monthly.

The FED makes calculations using measures to fill the holes, such as hours worked from the Employment Situation survey, or THE amount of power used by the industry in question during the month. The complete procedure for calculating the index is set in the best place to search for a detailed description of the methods involved - the 'Explanatory Pages' of the FED itself. Hundreds of components form the index, which is then identified as index level.

For example, the preliminary release of the September 2019 Industrial Production Index came in at 109.52. This reflects the current performance in relation to the base year. The FED had used 2012 as its base period at the time of publication. The level of 109.52 in September 2019, therefore, means that output rates in the reference period of 2012 were 9.52 percent higher than the average level. Manufacturing accounts for just approximately 20 percent of the U.S. economy but is closely controlled by F.X. and CFD traders.

The industrial sector is significant as it is responsible for much of the change in U.S. production seen in the business cycle, along with the construction sector, and can provide insights into the evolution of the structural economic changes. The Global Manufacturing Index is procyclical. That means agreement exists among its movements and the shifts in the business cycle. The link between this index and economic activity is sufficiently strong for some analysts to use this study as an early indicator of how GDP might be achieved.

Capacity Utilization:

This indicator assesses how the maximum potential of the U.S. manufacturing sector is going. The full capacity concept is the greatest level of sustainable production which a factory can achieve within a practical framework. In other words, it takes things like normal downtime into consideration. It is measured as an Industrial output index ratio divided by a maximum capacity index.

It offers us a timely indicator of manufacturing / economic safety, as well as an insight into patterns that may emerge within the manufacturing sector. This can also include hints about inflation. When plants run fast, it is a fair assumption that producers will increase prices. Unless the factories run above their full efficiency, computers are likely to malfunction due to overwork.

Taking offline computers raises the possibility of laying off staff at a time of high demand, which is expected. Consequently, by increasing costs, producers are able to cope with rising demand, rather than laying off workers. In addition, this is likely to feed into consumer prices, contributing to higher inflation. When, on the other hand, capacity utilization operates at low rates, it is a major weakness in the economy.

Generally speaking, rates below 78 percent have tended traditionally to point to an impending recession — or could even indicate that the economy is still in recession. As such, the FED uses this metric to monitor industrial patterns, the broader economy, and even inflation. This makes it an important indicator to monitor for CFD traders, particularly for bond traders, and it's also a key marker for all those involved in the equity and F.X. markets.

2.5 Market Psychology and the Golden Rule of Economic Indicators

Thanks to predictions and consumer sentiment, currency levels frequently start shifting just before the actual data comes out!

Sentiment analysis is a kind of F.X. analysis which focuses on indicating and therefore calculating the overall emotional and psychological state of all foreign exchange market participants.

This form of Forex research aims to measure which proportion of F.X. market players are bullish or bearish, that is to say, positive or pessimistic.

Markets are starting to switch from assumptions and predictions, which are also available in economic calendars. When the forecast promised positive growth, and the statistical evidence comes out even better than expected, it further amplifies the currency's rise.

This creates a significant downward pressure on the currency if the final data comes out worse than expected.

Economic factors that affect the value and intensity of a currency's value ultimately drive the forex market. A country's economic outlook has the greatest impact on the value of its currency. Learning the indicators and factors to monitor will help you keep up in the fast-moving, competitive forex environment.

Chapter 3: Role of Optimum Timing in Forex Trading

The Foreign Exchange market currently operates 24 hours a day, making it virtually impossible for a single trader to monitor any movement in the market immediately and respond at all times.

Currency trading is all about timing. It is necessary to consider how much liquidity there is around the clock to optimize the growth potential during a trader's market hours to formulate an appropriate and time-efficient investment strategy.

Apart from just liquidity, the trading range of a currency pair often depends heavily on geographic position and macroeconomic factors.

Understanding what time, a currency pair has the maximum or narrowest volatility in trading would certainly help traders increase their investment usefulness because of a better allocation of resources.

3.1 The Importance of Timing in Forex Trading

The forex market is open and available 24 hours a day, seven days a week, as you probably already know. Traders can log into a trading platform and transfer currency around at any time, but that doesn't automatically mean people will transact around the clock. Timing will also be critical when trading forex, as there will often be good times for trading and not-so-good times for trade. This chapter outlines the best times to trade forex and the occasions when it is well worth staying away from the market, to ensure you only trade at the optimal times.

While you can theoretically enter the forex market and trade during the forex trading week at any hour of the day, many traders find that some hours provide more liquidity and broader spreads than others.

In particular, during a time of instability like any pandemic-influenced economic climate, the volatile foreign exchange markets are sometimes fast-moving. All kinds of factors can influence market activity, including major central bank news releases or instances of political instability such as general elections. As a trader, when conducting your market entry and exit actions, you need to respond to those.

3.2 The Optimum Time to Trade Forex

Any session will begin with emotionally motivated movements triggered by political events. Also, sudden movements in the forex market that occur in Australia and Tokyo in the evening and late-night sessions may intensify later in either European or American sessions.

Numerous day traders make a habit of never taking positions overnight to avoid having to watch them in other sessions of commerce. Many traders who do keep positions overnight often tend not to trade on Sundays or at night.

Nonetheless, many momentum traders frequently take positions that they keep for more than one day. They also have rules to avoid selling during significant releases of economic data and other highly volatile periods.

Basically, as with other things in existence, when trading forex, timing is everything.

Many forex traders prefer a market with plenty of price action and where large volumes of a currency pair change hands to increase liquidity in the market.

These markets usually offer the most opportunities, especially for short-term trading strategies such as scalping or day trading.

Concerning the above, it is also fair that the forex trading periods that offer the most opportunities occur when several major forex markets are open and overlap with other large forex markets. You can see these times in here.

Another critical factor about trading hours is which of the big trading sessions would offer the best opportunity for currency pairs to make trades.

Because market conditions tend to differ between the major trading sessions for the major currency pairs, your choice of a trading period can depend on which currency pair you choose to trade-in.

Monday Afternoon:

When it comes to trade, Monday mornings can well be a time to stop, but Monday afternoons are a different thing altogether. It is because the economy is beginning to warm up, with the volume of trading growing. Once again, you can't expect the forex market to hit peak liquidity during this period, but when Monday afternoon rolls around, it's always worth taking a look at the market.

When Multiple Sessions Overlap:

London is ranked as the busiest trading session, with New York not far behind. If that is the case, you should expect the session's duration to be a busy time with plenty of trading opportunities. Many experienced traders (or at least those trading full-time) also find 14:00 GMT to be the best time to enter the market as it is the time when London is coming to close, and many are waiting for the move to New York City. Although market fluctuations during this period can be choppy and even erratic, the major swings open the door to greater profit opportunities.

Between 12:00 GMT and 07:00 GMT — while not as popular as London / New York — another difference between Sydney and Tokyo still proves to be a wise time to trade.

When the Liquidity Is High:

Markets pick up on Monday afternoons, but the forex market will not hit peak liquidity until the earliest Tuesday. In the middle of the week, the forex market is most notably active, mainly Tuesday mornings through Thursday. If liquidity is what you are looking for, make sure to keep the majority of your trading locked by mid-week, as it is when trading activity is at its peak.

During European Sessions:

Almost any trading session has the possibility to get extremely busy, but one remains far more active than all the other trading sessions. The European sessions are considered periods when trading peaks, with around 30% of all trading taking place during these hours.

3.2 When Not to Trade Forex?

There is no doubt that the positive outcome of Forex trading is built on a foundation of dedication and execution, from awareness to the creation of a trading strategy. Timing also plays a crucial role on top of that, perhaps a more vital function than most people know, enabling you to choose your moments. Here's a list of some times when should not be trading currencies to avoid any unforeseen losses.

Late Sunday or Early Monday:

Looking at one of the worst times to trade forex, nothing is more slumber-inducing than the crossover late Sunday / early Monday. All remain sluggish throughout this time and, in many ways, acts as a reassessment phase, with so many using the crossover to prepare for the week ahead instead of trading actively. When the new week dawns, the greater percentage of investors stop making trades, and it's safe to say you will do the same.

During Major News Releases:

Financial reports, legislative updates, and economic data drive the forex market, with the temptation to trade when those are gripping the market. When doing so, you may be at the center of the action, unless you have a strong understanding of how to exchange the news, staying away is advised. Updates, data, and reports, mainly when the news turns up unexpectedly, can have an unforeseen effect on the forex market. Track big news releases with an economic forex calendar to keep ahead of what is to come and not get caught out.

During Strange Price Action Times:

There'll be instances when a forex pair, without any noteworthy real logic, throws up strange price action. Random movements give the market an exciting feeling, but the rocky trading terrain is usually what they do. That means it can be incredibly hard to understand what triggers these price changes and general market sentiment. Thus, it is better to ride out the storm before the unusual market activity comes to an end when strange price action occurs.

When the Liquidity Is Low:

Low liquidity levels that plague Asian sessions are rightly a red flag. The amount of funds traded throughout Asian market sessions is often quite small, so the average pip moves are too low to cover the Asian currency's high spreads. It is especially true near rollover time at the end of the day.

Protect your money by not selling at the wrong time, and keep your confidence. Although recognizing when is the right time to evaluate the charts and make the bids is vital, knowing when to NOT open positions are equally important.

The inactive (often referred to as "thin") market provides smaller rate fluctuations, hence fewer future income. Regardless of the reduced liquidity, a thin market usually comes with higher commissions (spreads) on each exchange. Simply put: if you want to sell a currency, it's more difficult to find potential buyers, so the broker or bank has to raise the fee because it takes the risk of not finding a buyer quickly.

A clear example of volatile activity accompanies significant news events just before, during, and immediately after. The currency rates can fluctuate wildly and unpredictably in these periods of volatility, thus messing up trading by generating execution lags, causing stop-loss orders, etc.

3.4 Forex Trading and the Time Frames

The shortest time frame traders can begin to look at when their trading day starts are regular maps, even though you sell on a 5-minute time frame!

The most common approach of multiple time frame analysis is to use graphs to define the overall pattern and then use the hourly charts to assess different entry rates.

Those who can do an analysis on a one-time frame have a lot of "screen time" and have been educated by looking at a lower time frame chart to grasp the long-term market motions.

Traders need to know how to spot an overall trend and trade around that one accordingly to make money in the markets reliably. Typical clichés include: "trend trading," "do not battle the tape," and "the trend is your friend." How long, though, does a trend last? When are you expected to join or leave a trade? Which exactly does short-term trading mean? Here we dig further into the timeframes for trading.

Time Frames:

You may identify patterns as primary, intermediate, and short-term. Markets do exist simultaneously in several time frames, though. As such, opposing patterns may emerge within a specific stock based on the time frame being considered.

New or inexperienced traders usually lock in on a particular time frame, ignoring the more influential primary pattern. Additionally, traders can trade the primary trend but underestimate the value of refining their entries within an optimal short-term time frame. Continue reading to learn what time period you should be monitoring for the best trading returns.

A general thumb rule is that the longer the time span, the more sensitive the signals are given. The maps become more littered with false moves and noise as you dig down in time frames. Ideally, a more extended time period will be used for traders to identify the primary pattern in whatever they sell.

Once the underlying trend has been established, traders may use their preferred time frame to determine the transitional trend and a faster timeframe to define the short-term trend. Choosing which group of time frames to use is unique to each trader. Ideally, traders will select the main time frame they're interested in, and then select a time frame above and below to comply with the main time frame. As such, the long-term chart will be used to identify the pattern, the intermediate-term chart will provide the trading signal plus the short-term chart to specify the entry and exit. But one cautionary note is not to get caught up in the noise of a short-term chart and evaluate a trade over. Generally, short term charts are used to validate or refute a primary chart hypothesis.

Chapter 4: Getting Started with Forex Trading

The forex (FX) market has a lot of parallels with stock markets; however, some main differences exist. This chapter will show you those variations and help you start trading in Forex.

If you have planned to take a steal on forex trading, it has never been easier to enter currency markets with a wide variety of online brokerage platforms promising everything like spot trading to futures and CFDs.

A proper approach to forex trading is desired as with any new venture, and indeed more than is true with most ventures. While there may be several ways to begin in forex trading, it is essential to understand the key steps:

4.1 Gathering the Important Information

As with any new trading venture, forex trading requires some training before trying. Part of the educational process involves learning about the forex trading environment, but an important aspect is a knowledge about the type of person you are.

Trading, maybe particularly forex trading needs character traits not present in everybody. Forex trading requires a specific mix of features, including intelligence, courage, and discipline, and market or mass psychology insight, possibly particular adaptive expertise into market forces, and drive, determination, and patience. If you don't have the specific mix of features required to be a forex trader, this isn't necessarily a personal shortcoming. Not everyone is a dealer. Some people love art, while some are good at industry, some are good at music, and some are good at trading forex. Even if trading is for you, it will take patience, commitment, and experience to become a good trader.

The first step is to understand the essential basics of Forex. This book is written to deliver the basics of forex trading. Research currencies too. It involves basic currency knowledge and the nation or region that utilizes it, as well as the underlying factors shaping currencies. After that, read about technical analysis and how most traders rely on it for most of their decisions.

The forex market offers many opportunities to engage in trading. Brokers provide prototype accounts with all the dynamics of trading in real-time but without any cost or risk of loss. Use the demo account to test your expertise, increase it, and build and check your investment strategies. It makes complete sense that you'd be able to benefit reliably in a trial account before trading with real money. Indeed, you might sometimes hear that the psychology of real-money trading makes it a lot harder to profit when dealing with real money and real risk. Be vigilant during this time span. Learn how to exchange "on paper" before investing real money.

4.2 Choosing A Forex Broker to Start With

Like in any other market, there are several forex brokers to choose from. Here are a few things every trader should look for:

Low Spreads:

The spread, measured in "pips," also known as low spreads, is the differential between the purchase price of a currency and the price at which it could be sold at any given time point. Forex brokers do not charge any commission, so that's how they make money. By comparing brokers, you'll find the gap in forex spreads is as large as the gap in stock arena commissions.

Regulatory Bodies:

Unlike stockbrokers, forex brokers are typically connected to large banks or lending institutions due to the substantial capital they need to provide (leverage). Forex brokers should also be required to register with the Futures Commission Merchant (FCM), and the Commodity Futures Trading Commission (CFTC) regulates them. This and many other financial data and statistics about a forex brokerage can be found on its website, its parent company's website, or via the BrokerCheck website of the Financial Industry Regulatory Authority.

Extensive Tools and Research:

Forex brokers provide their customers with several different trading channels-much like brokers in other markets. These trading platforms often include real-time charts, technical analytics tools, real-time news and data, and even trading system support. Once subscribing to any broker, be sure to apply for free trials to check various trading platforms. Brokers also typically provide the technical and necessary information, economic calendars, and other analysis.

Leverage:

In Forex, leverage is essential because the price fluctuations (the sources of profit) are only fractions of one cent. Leverage, defined as a ratio of overall available capital to real cash, is the amount of money that a broker can lend you for trading. A ratio of 100:1 means, for example, that your broker will lend you $100 for every $1 of real money. Most brokerages sell 250:1. Note that lower leverage means lower margin call risk and lower bang (and vice versa) for your dollar.

If you have limited resources, make sure your broker provides high leverages through a margin account. If capital is not a concern, then any broker with a wide range of leverage options can do so. Various options allow you to vary the amount of risk you wish to take. For example, it might be better for notoriously risky (exotic) currency pairs to have less leverage (and thus less risk).

Many brokers offer two types of accounts or more. The smallest account is labeled as a mini account, which allows you to exchange at least $250, say, providing a high volume of leverage (which you need to make money with this initial capital size). The regular account allows you to trade at a number of different leverages but requires at least $2,000. Ultimately, premium accounts, which mostly require considerably higher amounts of capital, allow you to use a varying proportion of leverage and often provide added tools and services.

Things to Avoid:

Sniping and hunting-described as buying or selling prematurely near preset points-are unethical actions performed by brokers to maximize profits. The only way to determine which brokers don't do this is to talk to fellow traders.

The broker has a say on how much chance you take when you deal with borrowed money. As such, at their discretion, the broker may purchase or sell, which could be a negative idea. Suppose you have a margin account, and before you rebound to all-time highs, your position is taking a dive. And if you have sufficient cash to cover, some brokers will end up your place at that low on a margin call. That action can cost you a considerable amount of capital on their part.

Be sure to take due diligence before selecting a broker! Signing up for a trading account is similar to obtaining an equity account once you have decided to. The only significant difference is that you're expected to sign a margin agreement for forex accounts. The arrangement stipulates that you are dealing with borrowed money, and as such, the trader has the right to interfere in your trades to protect their interests. That said, you'll be able to trade once you sign in and fund your account.

The forex market is one of the world's largest markets, and individuals are becoming ever more interested in pursuing their FX trade. Before you start trading, however, there are various factors to consider, such as ensuring your broker meets specific criteria and the ability to understand a trading strategy that tends to work best for you. One way of learning to trade Forex is by opening and trying out a demo account.

4.3 Setting up An Account

Once you have done enough practice and feel confident, it is time to open a real account. Remember that you risk losing your money. You may start with micro or mini-sized account to reduce the potential loss (or profit).

Proceed and deposit to allow the trading with your account open. Mind starting small and using just the money you can afford to lose. When money lost means fewer funds are available for the necessities of living, such as food for yourself or your family, go back to the accounts of practice and wait until you are richer before joining the Forex.

Even if you're genuinely able to reach the forex market, ease it. Trade with caution; closely watch the currency pair and don't bring all your money to the market. Speak of the initial time and money spent in schooling as an income. At first, you could get lucky, but the initial margin account is more likely to be lost. Take the time you need. The forex market is not a scheme to get-rich-quick; it is learned only by time and practice.

It is with the experience that peace of mind arrives. Once you have that sense of security that you are capable of on the forex market, and since the trading experience and successes mount, the amount of trading increases slowly. Yet be still vigilant and disciplined. Even traders who have had experience lose money. Ensure that your marketing style works for you, and then stick to it.

4.4 Arranging the Money

Money is the most crucial factor in the beginning, and running a company and an entrepreneur must find ways to secure financing for a small business. There are many choices that an entrepreneur should look at when it comes to funding his small business and that each comes with its benefits and drawbacks.

The truth of life is that all reasonable goals are worthwhile. Mastering the skills of Forex trading is one of the goals we want to achieve, which takes considerable effort. Many good forex traders are there who only adapt to just how much money they want to make. They never think of forex trading as an activity that needs effort in its growth. It is human greedy and lazy nature, which often keeps people away from this fact. That's so many good brokers search for the new trading tools regularly. To get a spell that will make them instantly wealthy all night!

It's necessary to accomplish goals, but somebody has to go through an utterly ordinary routine. That's just writing down a "Wishlist" to make this work. Suppose we mention how many thousands of dollars we would like to make per month or week. And how many millions of dollars we want to make in a year or two!

One should compose a list like this without having to think twice. The consequence is nothing more than an amusing exercise. And everyone feels good to think about how much money will possibly be made in a short time!

The question isn't what the right set of targets is. Setting targets must include deciding how much commitment you need in it. Suppose daily exercise is based on the forex chart to recognize transaction opportunities. Placing a trade is a real process, including money loss and the development of stable mental behavior to master negative emotions from damages.

Here are some ways you can arrange money to get started with Forex Trading:

Self-Finance Your Venture:

One of the manageable ways to start and be a successful trader is to invest your own money in the market. There are no strings attached to your own money, and you can do pretty much anything you want. A company can be financed on its own by personal savings, but it has some drawbacks. You may not have the optimal amount of capital required to start the company, and there is always a possibility of using your savings to finance a company that may or may fail.

Bootstrap:

The investor can opt to bootstrap when a company is typically self-funded. This happens as the entrepreneur uses the cash that the company earns to keep it going and expand it. This is a perfect way to run a business because the owner retains full ownership of the company and does not have to pay any extra amount because interest comes with any loan you take. On the contrary, is the fact that capital is again limited and the market is increasing.

Acquaintances:

Often, an investor can raise money from his friends and relatives to start their company. This helps an investor to access a more considerable amount of capital without losing the company's power. This investment from friends and family is usually made on a personal basis, and the investor also charges no tax on the money he has earned. The entrepreneur must return the capital, however, and this kind of investment is not usually of a long-term nature.

4.5 Crucial Traits for a Successful Trade

Trading in Forex is not only about finding a strategy, putting it into practice, and then making loads of money. Regular traders acquire specific characteristics in all market environments, which then, in turn, allow them to execute a strategy effectively. When somebody starts trading, they're unlikely to possess all of these traits. They may be substantial but may need to focus on the other characteristics. That is good news. It means that there is no birth of successful traders; they develop through strenuous work that involves these traits.

Most traders start with the best of intentions. Still, their concentration too often gets misdirected, with too much attention being paid to achieving short-term targets or promoting themselves. There is not enough time spent looking at the mechanism and focusing on it. To the trader who wants to grow into adopting the mentality and mindset required to progress in the financial markets, we would recommend 'going' into a target or trying to apply the practice and integrate the ten characteristics into their overall approach to their work. The traits do not have a hierarchy. In many instances, the attitudes and actions associated with one trait tend to strengthen another: the overall aim of all these traits is to manage the trader to improve their self-efficacy and ability to succeed as traders effectively.

Discipline:

Discipline is a key characteristic that every trader needs. The market offers you endless opportunities for commerce. Every second of the day, you can trade thousands of different products, yet very few seconds offer great commercial possibilities. If a methodology generates about five trades a day and stops losses and targets for each trade are automatically set. During the day, there are only around five seconds of actual trading activity. Every other second is an opportunity to mess up those five trades, take up more trades than you should, get distracted or skipping trades, exit the trades you're in prematurely, or hold trades too long.

That doesn't just mean that your trades last 5 seconds. Five seconds of operation means placing an entry order takes only one second, and then you need to sit down on your hands again. It can take another second to change your stops and goals.

However, the bottom line is that your actual trading time is minuscule every day, even though you're an active day trader. You have to sit there, the majority of the time, focused, waiting for signals from the trade. When a trade signal occurs, you must act without hesitation, in accordance with your business plan.

Traders need the discipline to be doing nothing if there are no opportunities, but they need to be vigilant for possible opportunities. Then they need the ability to act immediately when opportunities to exchange arise. Once in a trade, traders are required to follow their trade plans with discipline.

Decisiveness and Mental Toughness:

The market is continuously throwing down losing trades at you, and you have to bounce back. If you feel discouraged whenever you lose a trade, or if your strategy fails to produce the result you expect, then your life will be miserable. Losing trades are constant; daily, most effective day traders will lose trades.

The difference between a thriving trader and an incompetent one is that most effective traders win on their winners slightly more than they lose on their losers and usually win somewhat more frequently than they lose. If your wins outweigh your losses, you may only need to win 30 percent or 40% of your trades.

Other traders may win 50 percent or 60 percent of their trades, but their wins may be equivalent to their losses or only slightly larger. In either case, trade-loss occurs. Despite these losses, daily profits can still occur, but only if you are not discouraged by the losing trades. If losing trades causes you to lose focus, the next trade, which could be a winner, is more likely to miss (or skip) you.

It also happens to lose streaks. Traders must stay concentrated and reasonable during a streak of failure and not let capital loss impact their judgment, making matters worse. It takes mental toughness to remain focused on executing your trading strategy and know when the market doesn't provide you with excellent strategic opportunities.

A trader has to withstand a continuous barrage of market punches. Losses are a trading fact, but this is how we act after some tough trades, which make all the difference. Follow your trading strategy after taking the losses, move on, and start. If you follow your plan but keep losing, business conditions are probably not right for your strategy. Step away in that situation, until they are. To be psychologically tough also means making the hard choice not to sell.

Proper Preparation:

It's challenging to find a trading book that doesn't emphasize particular virtues. Pursuing and exercising these virtues within one's trading is one of the most challenging things to achieve regularly. In a few moments of ill-discipline, all the hard work and preparation, which goes into one's work, can be lost. Successful traders place considerable emphasis on these trading aspects; they think thoroughly through what they do. Their planning and preparation provide a solid foundation that enables them to assert the required patience and discipline; it also helps to reduce uncertainty and thus helps to reduce levels of anxiety and stress. But, let's not pretend that active traders are anything like perfect in this field. However, they aren't, many of them will exhibit higher propensities to show these skills than most traders. Nonetheless, it is this ability to fulfill these abilities and qualities that put a trader in the proper spot to do well in the long term.

Embrace Risk and Uncertainty:

Successful traders have enormous respect and appreciation of the dangers of uncertainty. They also recognize the subtle difference between the two and work with it. Risk is only a small part of the uncertainty. Something is 'at risk' every time you trade. It is much more self-evident than 'uncertainty' as a concept. Uncertainty itself is much broader: it is impossible to value exactly how tomorrow's market will behave. Some people are trying to price uncertainty, which they mistake for risk, but it is difficult to put a real price on uncertainty. Admittedly, this point is contentious, and some may debate the simplistic definitions, but we do believe that attempts at price uncertainty typically end up in disaster. People thought they rightly valued uncertainty at LTCM. The experiences of this were soon forgotten as people also assumed, they had priced uncertainty well ahead of the global financial crisis. Top traders take on risk, and they respect uncertainty. They know crucially that they don't know what's coming next, and make educated guesses at best. Happy traders aren't gamblers. The only casino game that is usually played by successful traders is poker. They generally don't see poker as gambling because they can shift odds in their favor. The odds are too heavily stacked at them in all other casino games. A positive outcome must be expected, not merely an assessment of the direction of the market.

Developing the Winning Traits:

Most forex traders aren't born with all these traits, they have a few, and they have to work on the others rigorously. You will learn these characteristics, which is a good thing because you are deciding successful day trading and not just your genes. Most of us are susceptible to other weaknesses, but with strengths, we can counteract these, which will help us minimize the harm of our weaker qualities.

Take a detailed inventory of the qualities you need to improve on, and the strengths you have. Ideally, take this stock based on trading experience, as trading appears to reveal flaws and weaknesses that we did not realize we had. The personal inventory requires that you look at your discipline, perseverance, ability to adapt, mental toughness, independence, and forward-thinking.

Balance does not offer tax advice, savings, or financial services. The details will be given without consideration of any individual investor's investment goals, risk appetite, or economic circumstances and may not be suitable for all investors. Past success doesn't suggest potential outcomes. Investing entails risk like a possible principal loss.

Chapter 5: Risk Management in Forex Trading

You can have the world's best forex trading system, but you could lose everything without a strong forex risk management strategy in order. What is managing risk? Simply put: it's a system of thoughts that offer investors protection from the downside. This may include limiting the size of your trade lot, hedging, trading only at certain hours or days, and identifying when losses should be taken.

Unfortunately, these measures are not being implemented by many traders. Why then? Mainly because they love achieving big bucks using leverage to make risky investments, despite the high possibility of completely losing everything. And while many traders have been successful in exercising such trades with demo accounts, they are overly optimistic and unable to succeed in executing such movements for real. But responsible retailers are taking precautions.

5.1 Understanding the Risks in Forex Trading

The forex market enables the purchase and selling of currencies worldwide. The end goal of forex trading, like stocks, is to generate a net profit by purchasing low and selling high. The advantage of Forex traders is that they choose a limited number of currencies over stock traders who have to parse dozens of companies and sectors. Forex reserves are known as highly liquid securities due to the high volume of trading. Most foreign exchange trades comprise spot transactions, forward transactions, foreign exchange swaps, currency swaps, and options. However, there is plenty of associated risks with forex trades as a leveraged product that can lead to substantial losses.

Leverage Risks:

In forex trading, leverage needs a small upfront investment to gain exposure to significant foreign currency transactions, called a margin. Minor price changes can lead to margin calls where an additional fee is payable by the investor. Aggressive utilization leverage will result in considerable losses in large amounts of initial investments throughout volatile market conditions.

Interest Rate Risks:

Interest rate risk relates to the profits and losses generated by oscillations in forward spreads and forward-looking mismatches and maturity gaps between foreign exchange book transactions. This risk applies to currency swaps, straight forward, futures, and options. A common approach is to divide the mismatches into up to six months and the past six months, based on their maturity dates. To calculate the positions for all delivery dates, gains, and losses, all transactions are entered in computerized systems. Analysis and forecasting of the interest rate environment are necessary to forecast any changes that may affect the gaps that remain.

Transactional Risks:

Errors in the coordination, managing, and validation of orders from a trader (sometimes referred to as "out-trades") can lead to unforeseen losses. Often, even if an out trade is mostly the fault of the dealing counterparty institution, the trader/customer's recourse may also be restricted in seeking damages for the losses resulting from the account.

Country Risks:

The stability of the issuing country must be assessed when weighing the options to invest in currencies. Exchange rates in many developing and third world countries are fixed to a world leader like the US dollar. In that circumstance, central banks need to maintain sufficient reserves to maintain a fixed exchange rate. Due to many balances of payment deficits, a currency crisis can occur and result in currency devaluation. This can have a significant impact on forex trading and prices.

Because of the risky nature of the investment, if an investor believes that a currency will decline in value, they will start withdrawing their investments, further depreciating the currency. Those investors who continue to trade the currency will find their assets illiquid or incur dealer insolvency. As for forex trading, currency crises exacerbate liquidity hazards and credit risks aside from decreasing the currency's attractiveness.

5.2 Evaluating the Risks

When you enter the internet, the risk can become totally out of control suddenly, partly because of the speed at which a transaction can take place. Indeed, transaction speed, immediate gratification, and adrenaline rush to make a profit in less than 60 seconds can also cause a gambling impulse that many traders succumb to. Therefore, they may turn to online trading as a form of gambling, rather than treating trading as a serious business requiring proper speculative patterns.

Speculating, as a trader doesn't mean gambling. Risk management is the difference between gambling and speculating. In other words, you have some control over your risk with speculation, whereas, in gambling, you don't. Even a card game like Poker can be played with a gambler's mindset or with a speculator's mindset, usually with different results.

The resulting losses can be much higher than expected, given the wide range of associated risks with forex trading. Since trades are commonly leveraged, a minimum fee may become highly leveraged assets and huge losses. Besides that, there is indeed a significant amount of uncertainty associated with it, as many extrinsic aspects influence foreign exchange.

5.3 Coping Up with the Difficult Situations

Notwithstanding the risks, however, forex trading still comes with significant benefits. Risks are still involved in trading financial assets, which should have little effect on your returns as long as you are prepared.

Some risk management strategies are listed below:

Acknowledge the Odds:

Thereby, the first rule in risk management is to calculate the successful odds of your trade. You have to understand both basic and technological analyzes to do so. You'll need to understand the market dynamics you're trading in and understand where the probable psychological price trigger points are that a price chart can help you make your decision.

The next crucial aspect is how you control or handle the risk once a decision is taken to take the trade. Remember, if you can assess the risk, you will mostly be able to manage it.

It is essential to draw a line in the sand when stacking the odds in your favor, which will be your cut-out point if the market trades to that level. Your risk is the gap between the cut-out point and when you reach the market. Psychologically, before you even take the trade, you have to accept this right risk upfront. When you can accept the possible loss, and you are OK with it, then you can take the trade further into consideration. If you're going to bear the damage too much, then you don't have to take the trade, you'll be severely stressed and unable to be objective as your trade goes on.

Because the danger is the opposite side of the coin to be compensated, you can draw a second line in the sand, where you move your original cut-out line to protect your spot if the market trades to that level. This is called sliding up your stops. The second line is the price you split at, even though at that point, the market is cutting you out. When a break-even stop covers you, your risk has been effectively reduced to zero, as long as the market is very competitive, and you know that at that price, your trade will be carried out. Make sure the differentiation between stop orders, limit orders, and market orders are understood.

Control Your Losses:

Knowing when to cut down on trade losses is a powerful method of risk control. It can be done with a "hard stop," in which you use trading platform advanced technologies to lock in a stop loss beyond a certain level, or it can be done with a "mental stop," where you mentally and emotionally decide to restrict the drawdown you're willing to take on a trade essentially keeping a commitment with yourself to change course at a certain point. For either process, resisting the temptation to push your stop loss further and further away, as investment values decline, is crucial.

Use Correct Lot Sizes:

Broker advertisements make it possible to open a $300 account and use the 200:1 leverage to facilitate 10,000-dollar mini lot trading and double your money in single trading. But that is highly risky and misguided. When it comes to analyzing your lot size initially, starting small is best for new investors to allow greater versatility in managing trades.

Track the Overall Exposure:

While it's a great idea to use a reduced lot size, opening multiple lots with currency pairs might severely damage you. For example: if you're short on EUR / USD and long on USD / CHF, you're exposed to the USD essentially twice. So, if the USD tumbles, a double dose of misery will come upon you. Yet keeping your overall exposure restricted can reduce your risk and increase your long-term prospects for success.

Risk is inherent in any trade you take, but you can handle it as long as you can quantify the risk. Also, don't ignore the fact that you can magnify your risk by using excessive leverage concerning your trading resources and being intensified by a lack of market liquidity. Taking on any risk is the only way to achieve good rewards, with a moderate approach and decent trade habits.

5.4 Why Traders Lose Money?

A widely established reality is that a large number of forex traders crash. Specific websites and blogs go so far as to suggest that 70%, 80%, and sometimes more than 90% of forex traders lose money and end up leaving.

Let's find the assertion which follows. If it is true that the market can only go up or down in the long run, then using the simplest 1:1 risk/reward ratio, there have to be at least 50 percent winners, shouldn't it? And that's not there. This chapter discusses in favor of the concept that a trader is their own deadliest enemy, and that the root of most problems is human error. In short, the most significant explanation for losing money from Forex traders isn't rocket science. It is the very traders.

Financial trading, like currency markets, requires long and thorough multi-level preparation. Trading cannot begin without understanding market dynamics by a trader and an ongoing study of the ever-changing market climate. Here are some reasons as to why traders lose their money while trading.

Failure to Manage the Risks:

You can be a skilled trader and yet be wiped out by poor management of risk. Your main job is not to make a profit, but to defend what you have. As your capital becomes depleted, you lose your ability to make a profit.

To combat this danger and enforce effective risk management, position, and transfer stop-loss orders once you have a fair income. Use lot sizes, which are reasonable in comparison with your account capital. Above all, if a trade doesn't make sense anymore, get out.

Indecisive Trading:

You may often find yourself struggling with the guilt of trading. This situation arises when a trade you are opening is not instantly successful, so you start thinking to yourself that you have taken the wrong path. Then you close and reverse your trade, only to see the market return in the initial direction you chose.

You need to choose a course in this situation and stick to it. All the flipping back and forth will only make you lose little fragments of your account continuously at a time before your investment capital is exhausted.

Not Accepting the Mistakes:

Some trades simply aren't working out. Wanting to be right is human nature, but often you aren't. As a trader, you have to embrace that sometimes you're mistaken and move on, rather than trying to cling to the idea of being perfect and ending up with a trading account with zero-balances.

It's hard to do, but occasionally you have to admit you've made a mistake. Either you joined the trade for the wrong reasons or the way you expected it didn't work out. The right step to take, though, is to admit the error, discard the deal and move on to the next chance.

Chapter 6: Analysis to Predict the Market Fluctuations

Retail forex day traders use the Forex analysis to decide whether to sell or buy decisions on currency pairs. It can be of a scientific sort, using tools such as charting instruments. The use of economic indicators and news-based incidents may also be central.

6.1 Fundamental Analysis

Fundamental analysis is used to assess developments in the forex market by analyzing statistics such as inflation, unemployment levels, gross domestic product (GDP), and other economic data coming from countries. For example, a trader performing a fundamental EUR / USD currency pair analysis may find knowledge about the eurozone interest rates more useful than those in the U.S. Such traders will also wish to be on top of any significant news releases emerging out of each Eurozone nation to gage their economies' relationship to safety.

Fundamental analysis is a method of study of the financial markets for price forecasting purposes. Fundamental Forex analysis refers to the overall state of the economy. It examines various factors, including interest rates, wages, GDP, foreign trade, and production, as well as their relative effect on the value of the national currency to which they refer.

In Forex, as well as many other financial markets, the central principle of fundamental analysis is that the price of an asset can vary from its value. For this reason, in the short term, different markets can misprice a resource, overprice, or underprice it. Fundamentalists believe that the assets will ultimately always return to the correct level, despite being mispriced in the short term. The end goal of carrying out fundamental research is to discover an asset's actual value, equate it to the current price, and find a trading opportunity.

It also shows the main distinction between technical and straightforward analysis beautifully. Although technical analyzes pay little attention to everything other than the current price, fundamental research examines anything but the current price. While it is true that fundamental analysis in everyday markets may not be the perfect method for a short-term trader, it is also the fundamental Forex factors and how they've been analyzed that respond to what happens in the long run.

The essential study of FX is not just about comparing current data from single economic measures with previous data. Several economic theories surround fundamental Forex research, seeking to contextualize various financial data to make it comparable.

The most prominent economic theories of fundamental currency analysis supervise the notion of the parity-a market level at which currencies must be exchanged when modified, based on their local economic conditions, such as interest rates and inflation.

You may have noticed that from an average Forex trader's convenient point of view, news reports are the ones that produce market movements. How does this happen, and why? Financial experts observe several economic indicators because they can provide economical health hints.

You can consider these metrics in news stories and news sources. Many are released weekly, others are published monthly, and a few are released quarterly. These updates and changes can be monitored via our Forex calendar. Now let's compare the frequency of data updates with technical and fundamental analytics.

In the case of fundamental analyzes of currency trading, new data shows up every second in the form of a price quote. In contrast, fundamental indicators are published at most only once a week. Compared to the countries where it could generate at a potentially faster rate, capital flows progressively from countries where it accrues at a potentially slower rate.

All this relates to the stability and strength of an economy. When an economy is expected to stay stable, it will serve as an ideal prospect for foreign investment, as it is more likely to deliver higher returns on the capital markets.

Upon that thinking, investors would first have to turn their money into the country's currency in question to invest. Buying more of that currency will push demand and force the appreciation of the currency. Sadly, economics isn't that easy, which is why historical examples of stable economies that display weakening currencies are not exactly unknown. Currencies aren't like corporate stock, which directly represents the economic health.

Once economic reports are published, traders and investors may look in different economies for signs of strengths or weaknesses. If the market mood bends in one direction before the news releases, the price shifts before the announcement are regarded as a 'market price.' Often it creates some commotion about the actual release of data.

In comparison, extreme market volatility can occur when the market is uncertain whether the data results differ from what was expected. This is why Forex novice traders are usually advised when carrying out fundamental research to stay away from trading around the headlines.

Fundamental Analysis Indicators:

The three leading economic indicators employed by the fundamental analysis of Forex are interest rates, inflation, and GDP. Especially in comparison to other considerations such as retail sales, capital flow, trade balance, along with bond prices and several other macroeconomic and geopolitical factors, they are unbeatable by the amount of economic impact they can generate. Also, economic indicators not only are measured against each other over time but also correlated with cross-discipline and cross-border indicators.

Interest Rates:

Interest rates are an important fundamental indicator of the Forex analysis. There are many types of interest rates, but here we'll focus on central banks' nominal or base interest rates. Central banks create money, and then private banks borrow that money. A base or nominal interest rate is called the percentage or principle that private corporations pay central banks for borrowing currencies. Every time you hear the phrase 'interest rates,' people usually refer to that concept.

Manipulating interest rates - a large part of national monetary or fiscal policy - is one of the central banks' primary functions. This is because the interest rates are a significant economic leveler. Perhaps interest rates are more influential than any other factor, and they affect currency values. They can affect inflation, spending, trade, productivity, and joblessness.

Central banks generally want to boost the economy and attain a level of government-set inflation, so interest rates are lowered accordingly. This stimulates private banks and individuals to borrow and stimulate consumption, production, and the economy as a whole. Low-interest rates can be a good tactic but a bad one.

Long-term, low-interest rates could over-inflate the economy with cash, creating economic bubbles that, as we know, will sooner or later generate a toppling domino effect across the economy, if not whole economies.

To avoid this, central banks can also raise interest rates, thereby cutting borrowing rates and leaving less money to play around with banks, businesses, and individuals. In the changing interest rates, from a Forex fundamental analysis point of view, the best place to start looking for trade opportunities is in.

Inflation:

News releases over a period of time on inflation data on increases in the cost of the goods. Note that every economy has a degree of 'good inflation' that it considers. If the economy expands over a long period of time, so needs the sum of money in circulation, which is the concept of inflation. The trick is to make governments and central banks' balance themselves at that stage of self-setting.

Too much inflation tips the supply and demand balance in favor of supply, and the currency depreciates because it merely exists more than it is demanded. The other side of the coin for inflation is deflation. The value of money increases during deflation, while goods and services get cheaper.

It may look like a positive thing in the short run, but it can be a negative thing for the economy in the long term. Money is economic fuel. Less fuel is equated with less movement. Deflation can have a drastic impact on a country at some point, to the extent that there will be scarcely sufficient income to support the economy going, let alone drive the economy forward.

Gross Domestic Product (GDP):

Gross domestic product is the calculation of all goods and services generated by a country within a given time limit. It is thought that GDP is the best overall economic indicator of an economy's health. This may seem odd, particularly given that GDP is a measure of the supply of products and services, yet it has almost nothing to do with the demand for such products and services.

The general idea is that to make reasonable and accurate estimates require a great deal of knowledge about both supply and demand. It would be unwise to think both sides of the market are reflected in GDP. Hence, an increase in GDP without a corresponding increase in demand or affordability for the gross domestic product is the very opposite of a healthy economy, from a fundamental perspective of Forex analysis.

The three main economic indicators employed by the fundamental analysis of Forex are interest rates, inflation, and GDP. In comparison to several other factors such as retail sales, capital flow, traded balance, and bond prices and multiple functional macroeconomic and geopolitical factors, they are unbeatable by the amount of economic impact they can generate. In addition, economic indicators are measured against each other over time and correlated with cross-discipline and cross-border indicators.

It is essential to understand that many economic data have been released, which have a significant impact on the Forex market. Users have to figure out how to make Forex fundamental analysis an essential element of their trading strategy to predict market movements, whether they want to or not.

6.2 Technical Analysis

The technical analysis takes the form of manual as well as automated systems. A manual method usually means a trader analyzes technical indicators and interprets those data into a decision to buy or sell. An automated trading analysis means the trader "teaches" the program to check for specific signals and translate them into executing buy or sell decisions. Automated analyses may have an advantage over their manual equivalent because they are supposed to take the behavioral economies out of commercial decisions. Forex systems utilize past price fluctuations to determine where to head a given currency.

Technical analysis was established on the premise that the markets are unpredictable (nobody knows what's going to happen next). Still, at the same time, price behavior is not necessarily random. In other terms, mathematical chaos theory proves that there are recognizable patterns that appear to repeat within a state of chaos.

This sort of chaotic behavior takes the form of weather forecasts in nature. For example, most traders would agree that when it comes to forecasting exact price changes, there are no certainties. Successful trading is not really about being right or wrong: when the odds are in your favor, it's all about assessing probabilities and taking trades. Part of determining the probabilities involves forecasting the direction of the market and when / where to enter a position, but your risk-to-reward ratio is equally important.

Know, there is no perfect combination of technical metrics that will activate some form of covert trade policy. Effective risk management, patience, and the ability to regulate your emotions are the keys to effective trade. Someone can guess right and win every once in a while, but it's nearly impossible to remain competitive over time without risk management.

Whenever it comes to the global foreign exchange market, buyers and sellers of currencies decide the prices of one foreign exchange instrument over others on a real-time basis. At the same time, governments are managing the volatility of currency levels to maintain stability. Technical analysis can be instrumental in the foreign exchange markets as technical levels provide insights into the levels in which government interference is likely to occur.

Technical analysis involves support and resistance levels in which currency pairs happen to seek lows and highs. Yet, price momentum indicators often signal upward and downward, where exchange rates run out of steam.

At times when black swan events happen, technical analysis will collapse.

The over-the-counter market is the most competitive and widely traded arena in the foreign-exchange world. The OTC market is a global, decentralized venue for all aspects of exchanging one country's currency for another; it's also the world's largest. The average trading volume for April 2019 was $6.6 trillion a day. The OTC business operates 24 hours a day, except at weekends.

Futures currency pair markets are smaller but represent the price action on the OTC market. The futures market offers a window into demand patterns and the relative strength or vulnerability of one currency versus another when it comes to technical analysis.

Volume and Open Interest Metrics:

The euro versus the dollar currency pair is the most frequently traded foreign exchange partnership since both foreign exchange instruments constitute reserve currencies.

The dollar's weekly chart against the euro futures contract reveals the currency pair's market action as of late 2017. The bar diagram shows the weekly volume, which is the total transaction number. The line above volume is the total number of long and short positions or open value.

It appears to be a technical confirmation of a price pattern in a futures market, as volume and open interest rise or fall with the stock. When the indicators decline with rising or declining rates, it also means that a trend is running out of steam, and the

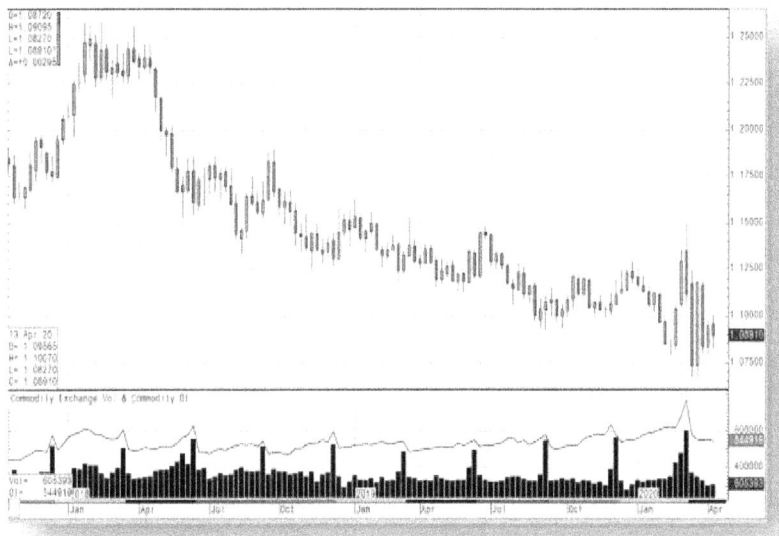

horizon may be reversing. Open interest and volume are the two technical metrics that help technical traders seeking signs that a trend is going to continue or change.

Momentum Indicators:

Stochastics and relative strength indices in a futures market will provide a glimpse into the overall power of a trend.

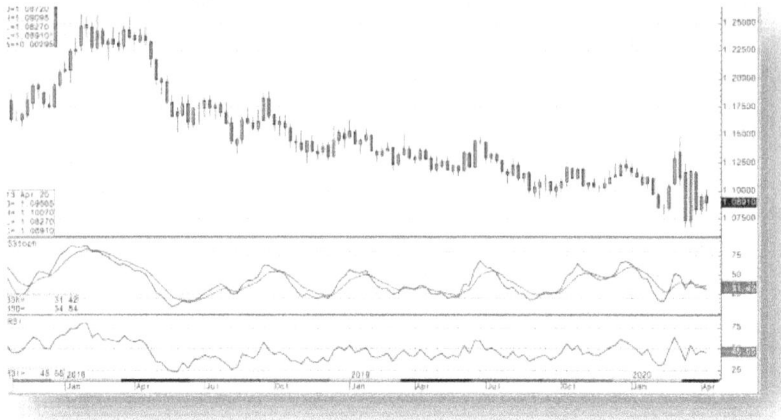

The slow stochastic below the weekly price chart is an oscillator aiming to measure the momentum of a price rise or fall — stochastics work by over time comparing price closures with price ranges. The idea behind this technical method is that prices continue to close in rising markets near the highs, and falling markets close to the lows.

A measurement below 20 indicates an oversold condition, while over 80 suggests an overbought situation. The interpretation of 31.42 on the euro's weekly chart versus the dollar currency pair showed that the stochastic oscillator is heading into oversold territory to indicate that the downtrend could run out of steam.

The relative strength index compares recent gains and losses to the basis of a market pattern, or the value. A reading below 30 is a sign of being over-sold, while an over-bought situation occurs with a reading over 70 rates. The indicator goes on to point to a neutral condition in the currency pair, at 45.55 on the weekly dollar versus euro chart.

Chapter 7: Tips for Maximizing the Profits and Minimizing the Losses

It is through diligence and discipline that the best traders develop their skills. They also conduct self-analysis to see just what drives their trades and to learn how to keep the equation out of fear and greed. Those are the skills that should practice every forex trader. Most newbie traders have a vision of getting rich in a matter of days. In reality, the journey to becoming a successful Forex trader requires hard work, patience, and practice. Yet don't despair, no matter how overwhelming that can sound!

7.1 Advice for the Newbies

Here is some advice for the traders who have just started and want success in their trading:

Understand Market Situations:

The significance of educating oneself on the forex market cannot be overstated. Take the effort to study currency pairs and what is affecting them before you risk your capital; it's a time investment that could save you a good amount of money.

Be Consistent with Your Plans:

The development of a trading plan is a critical component of active business. It should include your profit targets, the level of risk tolerance, methodology, and evaluation criteria. Once a plan is in place, make sure that every trade that you consider falls within the parameters of your plan. Remember: you're probably the most rational before placing a trade, and the most unreasonable after placing your trade.

Practice:

Put your strategy to the test with a risk-free demo account in real market conditions. You will get an opportunity to see what it is to continue trading currency pairs while also taking your trading plan for a trial run without risking your capital.

Predict the Market "Weather Conditions":

Fundamental traders tend to trade relying on news and other political and financial data; technical traders tend to forecast market movements utilizing technical analysis instruments such as Fibonacci retracements and other indicators. Many traders use a blend of both. Whatever your style is, you must use the tools available to find potential trading opportunities in shifting markets.

Know When to Stop:

You don't need to sit down every minute of every day and watch the markets. By stopping and limiting orders, you can effectively manage your risk and protect potential profits, and get you out from the market at just the price you set. Trailing stops are particularly helpful; as the market swings, they trail your position at a similar distance, helping protect profits should the market reverse. Contingent placing orders may not necessarily limit your risk of losses.

Analyze Your Limits:

This is simple yet critical to your success in the future, know your limits. This involves knowing how much you are willing to risk on every trade, setting your leverage ratio to suit your needs, yet never risking more than you can afford to give up.

Control Your Emotions:

You have an open position, and it's not the market that is going your way. You might be able to make that up with a swap or two that don't suit your trading strategy.

"Trading for vengeance" never ends well. Don't let the emotion in your successful trading strategy get in the way. Do not go all-in to try to make it back in one shot when you're having a losing trade; it's wiser to adhere to your plan and make the loss or damage back a little at a time than suddenly find yourself with two devastating losses.

Keep It Slow:

Consistency is one of the keys to commerce. Many traders have lost money, but if you establish a stable edge, there is a better chance that you will come out on top. It's nice to educate yourself and build a trading strategy, but the real test is by persistence and consistency sticking to that strategy.

Explore:

While consistency is important, don't be afraid to re-evaluate your trade plan if things don't work as you thought. As your experience continues to grow, your needs can change, your plan must always reflect your objectives. If your aims and objectives or financial situation are changing, then your plan should.

Don't Hesitate to Take Breaks:

Remembering to take some time off your screen is an easy practice to follow every day. This is particularly important when you're engaged in a long and taxing trading session. Analyzing multiple data streams across different windows of your computer will no doubt leave you feeling tense on occasions. It's effective to take breaks and walk away from the computer for some time when this happens. Spend some time to gather your thoughts. Upon returning to your office, you'll be calmer and better able to concentrate.

7.2 Tips and Tricks for Advanced Forex Traders

Forex trading can be a great way to diversify a more extensive portfolio or take advantage of specific FX strategies. Beginners and experienced forex traders need to remember that strategy, knowledge, and restraint are essential to getting ahead and staying on. Here we come up with some tips to bear in mind when thinking about Forex trading.

Define Your Goals:

Until setting out on some journey, it's essential to get a sense of your destination and how you're going to get there. Therefore, it is imperative to have clear goals in mind and then ensure that your trading method is capable of achieving those goals. What style of trading has a different risk profile which needs a certain attitude and positive approach to trade?

If you have funds that you ultimately benefit from the appreciation of a trade over a period of several months, you might be more of a trader in the position. Ensure that your personality fits the business style you engage in. A personality mismatch often results in stress and some losses.

Keep Your Expectations Realistic:

No trick or guide to forex trading will ensure consistent success. It would help if you accepted that every trade you do involves a risk of failure. You won't benefit from any decision, and no book or advertisement that tells you otherwise can trick you. Be realistic about your goals and targets.

Choose a Reputable Broker:

Choosing a reputable broker is of great importance, and it will be beneficial to spend time researching the differences among brokers. You need to know the policies of each broker and how they manage to create a market. Trading in the over-the-counter or spot market is different from trading the exchange-led markets.

Make sure your broker's trading platform is appropriate for the research you wish to make. For example, if you want to trade off Fibonacci numbers, ensure the broker's platform can draw Fibonacci lines. A good broker with the wrong platform or a good broker platform can be a problem. Check that, so you get the best of both.

Consistent Methodology is Crucial:

Before you approach any market as a trader, you should have insight into how you are going to make decisions to execute your business. You need to know what information you need to make the correct decision about whether to join or leave a trade. Some people look at the underlying economic dynamics and a chart to decide the best time to conduct the exchange. Others only use technical analyzes.

Whatever methodology you choose, make sure your method is adaptive and be consistent. Your system should stick to changing market dynamics.

Determine Your Entry and Exit Points:

Many traders get puzzled by conflicting information occurring when viewing charts in different timeframes. In reality, what appears as a buying opportunity on something like a weekly chart could appear on an intraday chart as a sell signal.

Therefore, be sure to synchronize the two if you take your simple trading course from a weekly chart and use a regular chart for time entry. If you get a buy signal from the weekly chart, wait unless a buy signal is verified in the daily chart too. Also, keep the timing coordinated.

Analyze and Calculate Your Expectancy:

Expectance is the formula that you use to assess how comfortable your program is. You can go back in time, calculate all of your winning trades and losses, and determine how successful your winning trades were relative to how much your falling trades lost.

Take a look at the last ten trades. If you haven't made any real trades yet, go back to where your code should have said you would join and leave trading. Determine whether you'd made a profit or a loss. Write down those results. Count all your winning trades and divide the result by how many wins you've made.

Don't Overtrade:

It's nice to be excited to learn a new skill, but there's a limit. Overtrading can lead to a lack of focus and sloppy trades. As you build your trading schedule, set the maximum number of trades per day or week, you will be doing.

Don't Be Greedy:

Greed will bring in unnecessary risks. Your trading plan must include the maximum acceptable loss and the profit you want. Stop trading once you reach either of those limits! This is among the most distinguished Forex tips when it comes to risk management for you to take away from this book.

Utilize Stop-Losses:

Our Forex tips and tricks are not merely about general recommendations. Also, worthy tools, such as the highly-rated stop-loss, are worth mentioning. Failure to set a stop-loss essentially gives you an argument to justify a lousy position open (because you secretly wish the situation will improve). But bad situations rarely recover, and if you don't wise up fast, neither will your capital.

A properly placed stop-loss removes the chance that all your money is lost on a single bad trade. The stop-loss is particularly useful when you cannot manually close the positions.

Analyze the Situation Weekly:

If the markets are closed, review weekly charts to check for trends or news that might affect your trade. Perhaps there's a trend making a double top, and the analysts and news indicate a turnaround of the sector. This is some kind of reflexivity where even the pattern could prompt the pundits, strengthening the pattern. You'll be making your best plans in the bright light of objectivity. Wait for your installations, and learn to be patient.

The above tips will lead to a standardized trading strategy, which will help you become a more sophisticated trader. Trading is an art, and the only proper way to become more professional is through constant and disciplined practice.

Conclusion

If your forex targets are ambitious (such that it will come to represent an essential component of your income or even the lion's share), then you should treat forex as though it were a company. You'll need to adopt an organized approach, in other words. Forex shouldn't be something you seek to get in whenever you feel like it; instead, you should strive to set aside a specific amount of time and incorporate forex into your daily routine. It would help if you devoted your time solely to education and research, unlike when you trade and track your account. Ideally, you might want to leave this kind of homework for the weekends if you are not distracted by live markets and the possibility of doing business.

A business also needs its own space. You might also consider getting a separate computer devoted exclusively to forex-related operations, depending on your forex regime's rigor. Forex isn't like your 9-to-5 job, which is probably interrupted by checking your Facebook account and espn.com frequently. It's Forex time when your laptop computer is powered on.

Ultimately, you'll have to control your forex company finances. All expenses should be reported with due care, and you should try to measure the return on investment for all costs, including this book! You will conduct an analysis of your account at monthly, quarterly, and yearly intervals. You will be able to display the productivity and efficiency metrics in real-time if you maintain a trading log. Did the result fulfill your expectations? If so, consider withdrawing from your account a fraction of your profits so that your earnings become real, not just digital. If your performance has been unsatisfactory, what can you do to make it better?

Remember, it will take time for your forex business to develop, as is the case with any new business. Give yourself a reasonable period of time in which you hope to succeed. Profits won't come immediately, but your forex company will one day be able to stand on its own two feet with hard work!

Success in Forex trading needs not only research but also understanding, not only preparation but also execution, not only achieving profits but also minimizing losses. Luckily, now you're well on your way to being an expert or becoming a good currency trader.

Our main adjective in writing this book was to provide you with a robust framework and base of knowledge to interact with the forex markets. Then it is up to you to apply for your experience. Good luck and take things slowly!

www.ingramcontent.com/pod-product-compliance
Lightning Source LLC
Chambersburg PA
CBHW051537240526
45465CB00027B/595